CROCHET FOR I _ _ _ _ _ _ _
2 BOOKS IN 1

The Most Complete Step-by-Step Guide
to Learn Crocheting Quickly and Easily
with Pictures and Illustrations, Including
Amigurumi and Amazing Pattern Ideas.

Cindy Watson

Contents

BOOK 2 - AMIGURUMI PATTERNS FOR BEGINNERS

BOOK 1

Crochet for Absolute Beginners

A Complete Step-by-Step Guide to Learn Crocheting and Create Your Favorite Patterns Quickly and Easily. Including Illustrations and Simple to Advanced Patterns

Introduction

If you are looking forward to learning crocheting, then this is the best book for you. It will introduce you to the crochet tools, the yarns, the hook, and the types of crochets. You will learn how to hold the hook and the yarn and then proceed to the techniques and stitches. In the end, you will be able to come up with successful projects that will motivate you even further into trying some amazing patterns.

Crocheting is a subject that attracts the attention of many people. It offers the simplest way with which people can express their creativity. As a result, when you go online, you will get plenty of books on crocheting. I would like to thank you again for choosing this one! We gave it all our efforts to ensure that it is as full of useful information as possible. Have some fun and enjoy it!

Learning how to crochet provides the most amazing experience. Rather than just spending your time on phones or other electronics, you can spend it on coming up with something more useful. crocheting will offer you the best way with which you express your creativity. You will have wide options for color choices and designs, and the way you will use them will express your ideas and thoughts.

By simply coming up with amazing designs that people admire, you will develop or boost your self-esteem because it will give you some sense of pride and the desire to achieve even much greater.

Teaching children how to crochet can be very important in improving or guiding them on following instructions, knowing how to read, understanding different colors, and even improving their mathematics skills through different crochet patterns.

Crochet is probably one of the cheapest and easiest hobbies. The very basic tools for crocheting include yarn and hook, but you also need to know more about other tools that will make everything easier. To get started, you need to prepare the following tools.

The very important thing that you must have is the yarn. Crochet is a yarn craft, and therefore, you must have the yarn. The yarn is what you will use for creating the fabric of your first project. Generally, there are so many yarn choices in the market, and it may be easy for you to get carried away. In the market, yarns are categorized according to their fibers (natural fibers, synthetic fibers, or a blend of both), colors, textures, weights, eco-friendliness, etc. You should not be overwhelmed by these categories.

For a beginner, it is advised that you avoid expensive yarns. Inexpensive yarns should be your friend. You should also avoid slippery yarns as well as anything with texture. As a beginner, textured yarns will make everything hard because it will be difficult for you to see your stitches. You are likely to be frustrated when you are not able to see your stitches. It is therefore recommended that you use smooth acrylic yarn that has a medium weight.

As a beginner, when buying yarn, be sure to choose a yarn with the number 4 symbol on its wrapper. Wool is also another fiber option that best fits beginners. However, the only disadvantage of wool is that it is more expensive when compared with acrylic. Cotton is the best natural fiber option. I prefer that you choose cotton because with it you can see your stitches. Often most people confuse between knitting and crocheting. The difference between these 2 is that you will use 2 pointed needles with knitting, while in crocheting, you will only use them on a curved hook.

When you go to the market, you will probably meet many hooks, including handcrafted hook, aluminum hooks, plastic hooks, bamboo hooks, ergonomic hooks, etc. Choosing a crochet hook can be a very difficult task, especially when learning how to crochet. This is because there are different crochet hook types and sizes. All that matters is that you get to find the set that best fits you.

However, you have to try different crochet hooks to determine the one that best works for you. This is the main reason why, as a beginner, you should have a set of them. Most sets especially set meant to be used by newbie crocheters, come with a range of different sizes for guiding them through some of the most basic patterns.

These hooks will range from small-sized hooks to large-sized hooks and work differently with different yarns' weights. The size of your crochet hook will determine your gauge. There is a complete beginner's set that I prefer you give to start with and then experiment with different types. With time as you will get to crochet, you will get to know your best crochet hook that you feel comfortable working with. Therefore, as you start, experiment with different hooks.

Furthermore, when buying a hook for a particular yarn, it is good that you make sure that the size of the hook matches the size suggested on the yarn label. It is recommended that as a beginner, you need to have a chart guiding you on how to pair different hook sizes and different yarn weights for your project.

Chapter 1: What You Need to Get Started

Take note that if your stitches are too tight or too loose, then your finished project might be slightly different from that of the pattern. If you have tight stitches, you can choose a bigger hook size, and a smaller hook size if you have loose stitches—for now. Try to produce even stitches that are not too tight or too loose. Practice makes perfect, and you will surely enjoy every minute of it.

Here are those materials and tools that you need.

Your Yarn or Thread

Crochet yarns come in different categories and thickness, and you need to use the correct hook size according to the thickness of your thread or yarn.

In the given chart below, the one used is 2 instead of 4. Assuming that you followed the right hook size to use and the given number was far off the number of stitches on the crochet gauge, it only means that you have a problem with the tension of your stitches.

If you have more stitches than the number of stitches indicated on the crochet gauge, then your stitches are too tight. To create balance, you can use a bigger hook size than the one suggested.

If you have fewer stitches than the number of stitches on the crochet gauge, then your stitches are too loose. You need to use a smaller hook.

Usually, the crochet gauge and the hook size are printed on the yarn label. It is recommended that you choose a cheaper yarn as your practice yarn. It is prudent to choose cheaper yarn since you are still in the learning stage. It is equally wise to choose light-colored yarns; you will see your error (just in case) and make necessary adjustments.

The chart below can help you understand and give you an idea about the different crochet threads and hook size to use.

Crochet Hook and Yarn Weight Chart

Yarn Weight Symbol and Category Name	0 LACE	1 SUPER FINE	2 FINE	3 LIGHT	4 MEDIUM	5 BULKY	6 SUPER BULKY	7 JUMBO
Other Names for Yarn in Category	Fingering, 10 Count, Crochet Thread	Sock, Fingering	Sport, Baby	DK, Light Worsted	Worsted, Afghan, Aran	Chunky, Craft, Rug	Bulky Roving	Jumbo Roving
Recommended Hook Size (US)	Steel[3] 6, 7, 8 Regular B-1	B-1 to E-4	E-4 to 7	7 to I-9	I-9 to K-10.5	K-10.5 to M-13	M-13 to Q	Q And larger
Recommended Hook Size (Metric)	Steel[3] 1.6-1.4 mm Regular 2.25 mm	2.25-3.25 mm	3.5-4.5 mm	4.5-5.5 mm	5.5-6.5 mm	6.5-9 mm	9-15 mm	15 mm and larger
Yards per 50 Gram Roll	275 yds	185-230 yds	145-180 yds	120-142 yds	100-120 yds	85-100 yds	70-85 yds	60 or less yds
Yards per 100 Gram Roll	545 yds	370-460 yds	290-360 yds	240-284 yds	200-240 yds	170-200 yds	140-170 yds	120 or less yds
Number of Single Crochets in 4 Inches[1]	32-42 double crochets[2]	21-32 sts	16-20 sts	12-17 sts	11-14 sts	8-11 sts	7-9 sts	6 sts and fewer

1 These are Guidelines only. They reflect the most commonly used hook sizes for crochet projects based on yarn category.
2 Lace yarn is usually crocheted on larger hooks to create open lacy patterns. Always follow the gauge stated in your pattern.
3 Steel crochet hooks are sized differently from regular hooks. The higher the number the smaller the hook, reversed from regular hook sizing.

Crochet Hook Size Chart

Here is a chart that can give you an idea of the kind of hook you can use for each yarn type. Just focus on the hook's size (some shafts presented in the chart are longer or shorter than the actual); the shafts of the different hook sizes have the same lengths, depending on the manufacturer.

Crochet Hook Conversion Chart		
Metric	**USA**	**UK**
2.00 mm	-	14
2.25 mm	1 / B	13
2.50 mm	-	12
2.75 mm	C	11
3.00 mm	-	11
3.25 mm	D	10
3.50 mm	4 / E	9
3.75 mm	F	-
4.00 mm	6	8
4.25 mm	G	-
4.50 mm	7	7
5.00 mm	8 / H	6
5.50 mm	9 / I	5
6.00 mm	10 / J	4
6.50 mm	10 1/2 / K	3
7.00 mm	-	2
8.00 mm	-	0
9.00 mm	15 / N	00
10.00 mm	P	000
15.75 mm or 16mm	Q	-

Steel Hook Chart (thread hooks)		
Metric	**USA**	**UK**
.6 mm	14	6
.75 mm	13	-
.70 mm	12	5
.8 mm	11	-
1 mm	10	4
1.15 mm	9	-
1.25 mm	8	3
1.50 mm	7	2.5
1.6 mm	6	-
1.7 mm	5	-
1.75 mm	4	2
1.85 mm	3	-
1.95 mm	2	-
2 mm	1	1
2.25 mm	0	00
3 mm	00	-

Steel and aluminum are the usual materials for the hook. Some crochet hooks come in bamboo, plastic, and combinations of different materials. You can choose any hook material, but just make sure you choose the hook with a nice hold. There are cheap crochet hooks and expensive crochet hooks with fancy designs, but it is best to start with a cheap hook.

Choosing Your Crochet Hook

As mentioned before, a novice should choose the F, G, H, or I U.S. hook size, and fine to medium thread. Look at the crochet hook size chart to see the different hook sizes and their material. First, take a detour in learning the proper way to hold your hook and the different grips.

Types of Crochet Hooks

So, you've seen the chart and the grips. But what are these hooks about, and what else should you know about them? Read on and find out!

Aluminum : Aluminum hooks are quite flexible. They are available in a vast amount of sizes and make crocheting quickly, and smoothly!

Steel : Steel hooks are best used for small objects and are often partnered with fine thread. Steel hooks are also known as thread hooks. Examples of crafts you could make with them include doilies and handkerchiefs.

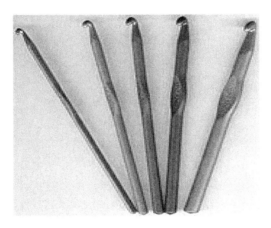

Bamboo : Meanwhile, bamboo hooks are known to be warm and lightweight. They could either be small, or large, never in between.

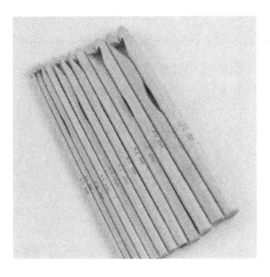

Plastic : Plastic hooks could often be common sized or jumbo. They're usually made with plastic that's hollow and are also lightweight.

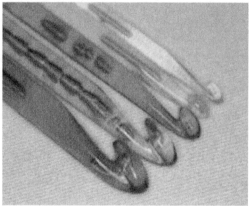

Tunisian : Finally, you have Tunisian hooks. They're longer than regular hooks. Sometimes, Tunisian hooks are called Cro hooks. They're known for having hooks on both ends, and that's why they're sometimes not recommended for beginners. Tunisian hooks are usually used to make crafts that are in the same mechanism as knitted projects. This means that the fabric doesn't look the same as normal crocheted projects do. This is because the stitches stay on the hook while you're making the project, instead of being on the canvas itself.

Things to Remember

1. Remember that crochet hook sizes are not universal. This is why you have a metric, U.S., and English sizes, and others, too. Remember that size always depends on the country where the hooks were made, the brand, and the material.

2. The shaft's diameter often determines size. The shaft is the point between the needle and the hook. This will then help you understand how big your stitches shall be.

3. The best thing to keep in mind about size is that hooks made in the U.S. are represented by letters in their sizes. The farther the letter in the alphabet, the larger the hooks get.

4. Remember that steel hooks best work with lace thread. Take note that as the number gets smaller, the hooks get larger.

Tapestry Needle

Some projects require you to sew your work, and you will need a tapestry needle for that. You can also use the tapestry needle to sew a crocheted appliqué to your project to make the project more appealing. The needle is typically larger than the average needle for sewing and has a rounded (blunt) tip. It has a threading eye to accommodate any yarn, although it may not work for bulky threads. While often used for cross-stitching, tapestry needles prove useful for crocheted materials, too, especially if you need to put on more detail on your project.

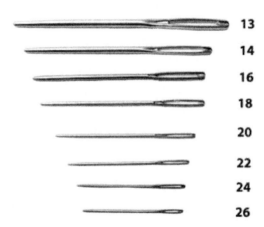

As you may have noticed, the larger the needle, the smaller the number gets, so don't get confused into buying a largely numbered needle thinking it would be a small-sized one.

Choosing Tapestry Needles

Now, you may wonder how exactly you'd choose your tapestry needles. Well, the general rule of thumb here is to make sure that you use the kind of needles that will easily accommodate whatever yarn or thread you're currently working with. This means that you'd have to use the smallest needle available, but not necessarily the smallest one out of all sizes because this would do nothing good for your fabric.

Scissors

To give your thread a clean-cut, you need a pair of scissors. It does not need to be an expensive pair, just the one that is sharp enough to cut your thread without trouble. Make sure to maintain your scissors properly.

As for crochet scissors, one of the most recommended ones is Stork Embroidery Scissors. They're amazing because they do not leave unhinged threads on your project, and would make your crafts neat as could be. Even stitches in front of your fabric will be neatly removed. A sample is shown below.

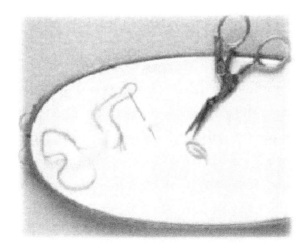

Stitch Markers

The usual stitch markers look like key holders, paper clips, small plastic hoops, and tiny padlocks. The markers are useful in keeping track of the start or end of a round in the pattern with repetitive instructions.

The marker can also serve as a reminder of the number of stitches that you have made so far. You can also use the markers to keep track of the round that you are currently crocheting. You can use improvised markers like pieces of thread that you can loosely tie around the post of your stitches on your current round, safety pins, and/or plastic rings. You can use different combinations of materials to mark different rounds

Crochet Hook Case

Your most important tool is your hook. It is best to keep your hook inside a case to avoid possible damage to the tip. There will come a time when simple patterns are not enough to hone your craft. Some projects only work well with a certain type of yarn and you will need a different hook for that. You might even find yourself owning more than 2 hooks and you need to store them in a case and keep them organized.

Chapter 2: Terms and Abbreviations About Crochet and How to Read Them

Abbreviations

Many times, this includes instructions for working special stitches. If a crocheter doesn't understand some of the stitches used in the pattern, the abbreviation is a good place to look for help.

Many abbreviations are standardized, so as crocheters gain practice reading patterns, they learn to immediately recognize single crochet for single crochet, dc for double crochet, and so on.

U.S.	U.K.
The chain(**ch**)	The chain(**ch**)
The single crochet(**sc**)	The double crochet(**dc**)
The half double crochet(**hdc**)	The half treble(**htr**)
The double crochet(**dc**)	The treble(**tr**)
The treble crochet(**trc**)	The double treble crochet(**dtr**)

Make sure you pay attention to the terms used before purchasing patterns.

Reading crochet patterns can be fairly time-consuming at first, but you'll get used to it. Patterns are written in rows for items that are straight and flat, such as a square cloth. For something like a coaster, the pattern is written in rounds, this is the terminology we use.

Here is a row to practice reading—Row 1: Chain 12, dc in 2nd chain from the hook and across in each. Chain 1, turn (9).

Firstly, you can see that this is part of a straight, flat item pattern because the pattern refers to row 1. Next, chain 12 indicates that this is a chain made up of 12 chain stitches. After this, there will be the half double crochet in chain number 2 from the hook (excluding the one carried by the hook). The half double crochet follows this in each stitch till the end of the row. Then you'll make one chain stitch for the following row.

Ready to try another one? This time we'll look at using asterisks. Here we'll focus on what part of the pattern needs to be repeated. Leave a piece of the long thread, chain 21. Sc in the 2nd chain and each across. (20 sts)—approximately 5" wide.

Row 1: *single crochet in first st, double crochet in the next* repeat till the end. Chain 1 and turn (20 stitches).

Leave a long piece of yarn, then start your chain which will be 21 stitches long. Next, make a single crochet in the 2nd ch stitch from the hook (exclude the stitch with is attached to the hook) and single crochet in each chain until the end of the row. It should be approximately 10-inch wide.

In row 1, read the pattern carefully. You'll notice that there are only 2 asterisks. Everything in between the asterisks needs to get repeated till where the row ends. Firstly, the single crochet is done in the first stitch, then the double crochet is what follows in the next. Single crochet in the first stitch comes again and is then followed by the double crochet. Follow through till the row ends. Make 1 chain stitch so that you can begin a new row.

This is just one example; you will learn as you go along. In addition to reading written patterns, you will also be able to use symbols to read patterns. Below is an elaborate list of common crochet symbols that are commonly used.

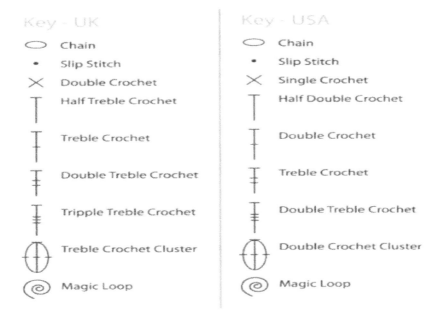

Instructions

The instructions are the pattern's meat, the place where the designer tells the crocheter what to do to make the item. For the most part, designers are explicit—"Chain 3, work 3 for turning chain, double crochet into the 3rd chain from hook"—but a few common shortcuts are used as well, including:

Asterisks

Asterisks are used to indicate repeats of patterns. A pattern might read: "Chain 1, slip stitch into the 2nd chain from hook, *3 single crochet, ch 2, 3 single crochet*, repeat from * to * 3 times, chain 1, turn." The stitches within the asterisks are repeated 3 times in the sequence they're given after the first time they're worked. So, in total, the asterisk would be repeated 4 times.

Parentheses

Parentheses are used to indicate repeats, often within asterisks, the crocheter might see: "...*3 single crochet, (ch 2, single crochet) twice, 3 single crochet*, repeat from * to * 3 times." To work the directions inside the asterisks, the crocheter would work 3 single crochet, 2 chains, 1 single crochet, 2 chains, 1 single crochet, then 3 more single crochet. Then the crocheter would repeat the instructions inside the asterisks the number of times called for.

Many crochet patterns are broken down into rows (for flat crochet) and rounds (for circular crochet). Pattern repeats are often made up of several rows or rounds, which the designer will indicate in the pattern. At the end of the pattern, the designer will include any special finishing instructions, such as adding embellishments or borders.

New crocheters should remember that although these are common conventions used in pattern writing, there are exceptions; designers are individuals, and some have their unique way of writing instructions.

Gauge Your Knitting

How do you know how many stitches you are going to use? Well, take a look at your yarn label. You will see a guide that says something like "5 sts = 1 inch on #6 needle."

Therefore, if you want your scarf to be 6-inch wide, you would need 30 stitches. If you followed my instructions and are using a larger needle, there are 2 ways to figure out the required number of stitches. You could guess how many stitches you should have, but that might mean you knit for a while and then determine the scarf is too narrow or too wide. If it is too wide, you could run out of yarn before reaching your desired length.

The best way to make sure you get the right width is to knit a small sample. I like to use 12 stitches for my samples because it breaks down into simple multiples: half = 6 stitches; third = 4 stitches; quarter = 3 stitches. That way, when I measure the width of the finished sample, it is easier to calculate how many stitches I have per inch more accurately. You need to know how many stitches per inch to multiply that number by the number of inches in width that you want.

For example, if you knit a sample using 12 stitches and your finished sample's width is 3 inches, you are knitting this yarn on these needles at a gauge of 4 stitches per inch. If you want a scarf that measures 6 inches wide, you would need to work 24 stitches (6 inches X 4 stitches/inch).

Blocking Mat

A blocking mat is something of which you might or might not be used. This relies on the crocheting activities you intend to do. Blocking is a method used in crocheting as well as in knitting. It includes dampening the thread, then molding it in a certain manner.

When you're crocheting you intend to do some blocking strategies, you'll want to buy a blocking pad. It should make that blocking a bit easier for you. It provides you with a good and durable surface to do your task.

This is not a necessary crocheting instrument but you must be aware of it. Without such mats blocking techniques can be used but getting the mats would make it much easier. Mats like that are also beneficial for many other arts and crafts projects. Buying any of these will be worthwhile, and having them around your residence.

Casting On

The first step to knitting is called "casting on". This is done by creating the first row of stitches on your needle. This is your foundation and will become one side of your scarf, so it is important to make it neatly.

There are many methods of casting on. Some types are more suitable for specific projects, but the long-tail cast-on is most common. You will never go wrong by mastering the long-tail cast-on technique!

In the example above, we determined that the 6-inch scarf requires 24 stitches for the width. Start by measuring a piece of yarn. Allow 1–2 inches for each stitch you will be casting on.

If you are using a Bulky or Chunky yarn and big needles, you will need 2 inches per stitch (48 inches, or 4 feet). If you are using a finer yarn and smaller needles, you will be fine with the 1-inch estimation. I usually add about 6 inches to my total, just to be safe. Do not cut the yarn. Just hold it where you have measured your desired length.

Step 1: Make a slip knot at the place where you have marked the length of your yarn for casting on. Slip the loop over one needle and pull the tail to tighten it.

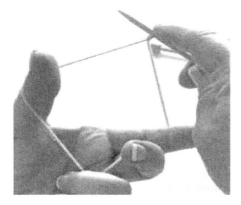

Step 2: Hold the needle in your right hand with your index finger on top, holding the slip knot in place.

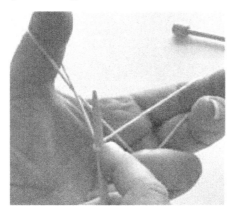

Step 3: With your left hand under the needle, wrap one strand around your index finger and the other around your thumb. You should have a triangle shape with your needle at the top point and your 2 fingers making the triangle base's 2 points.

Step 4: Bring the needle down so the yarn makes a "V" between your thumb and forefinger, which are now positioned like you are pointing a gun.

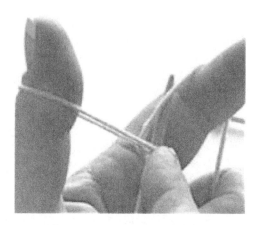

Step 5: With your right hand, guide the needle's tip under the left side of the yarn that is looped around your thumb.

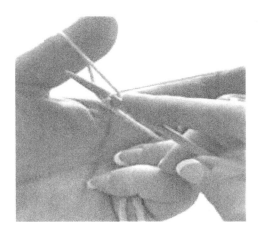

Step 6: Guide the needle UNDER this point and OVER the yarn on the right side of your thumb.

Step 7: Move the tip of the needle OVER the left side of the yarn on your index finger.

Step 8: Swing the needle back THROUGH the loop on your thumb.

Step 9: You will see that you have a loop on your needle now. Pull your needle up and release the yarn on your finger. Then pull the 2 yarn ends to tighten the cast on stitch.

The cast follows this pattern: under your thumb, over your index finger, and back through the thumb loop. Use this as your cast-on mantra: UNDER-OVER-THROUGH, UNDER-OVER-THROUGH...

Congratulations! You have your first stitch. I think casting on is the most complicated part of knitting a scarf. Once you master this, the rest will be easy. Cast on the remaining number of stitches that you need for your scarf.

Stitch Markers

For the more advanced you may want to consider stitch markers. They allow you to mark the start and endpoints of your work. They also come in handy when crocheting round patterns.

Chapter 3: How to Work Crochet for Right-Handed People

The whole process of crocheting commences with a candid and easy understanding of slipknot. From this, it can graduate into something beautiful both to the eyes, and that is pleasing. Various items result when crocheting. It could be a hat or a table cloth or even a blanket. All these factors are dependent on the type of string that you choose. When you are at the beginning of knowing how to crochet, this process can be less subtle when you employ fine yarn.

When crocheting as a right hand, you may choose to use single crochet or double crochet. The procedure, however the same has some distinctions. First, we are going to look at how crocheting with single crochet works.

Crocheting With a Single Crochet

The sizes of crochets vary. There is a 7-inch and you can also find a 9-inch. This is because of the discrepancy of the various sizes of the intended purpose. When using the right hand, there are various steps that you need to follow to make sure that your crocheting is worthwhile.

Your initial stage is making sure that you take the crochet by the right hand, and on the hook, you will make a slip knot. After this, you need to make sure that the yarn is brought towards the front from the back. Do this, and they make sure that you have held the yarn inside the hook. After which you will have achieved the one chain stitch.

What commences the whole crocheting process? This happens when you move the yarn, which is hooked onto the hook via the slipknot. To achieve further chains, you need to do this process repetitively until you have various strain chains.

After this, you can now miss the first chain stitch. You will then take the hook and put it at the epicenter of the following chain stitch. Pull the yarn from the chain stitch and then up to the hook. After this, you will have achieved 2 loops on the hook. You are now in a position to yarn over from the rear to the front. Here one loop will stay on the hook, and as a result, you will have achieved the single crochet stitch.

Do this for a maximum number of 5 and 6 times in one of the other chains to finish a single crochet row. When you are where the row is at its end, make sure that you make a total number of one chain stitch. After you have achieved this, you can now turn your work in a clockwise manner to make sure that you leave the hook inside the chain. This is to help maintain the flow.

After you have achieved this, you can now commence on the following chain. To achieve this, you need to make sure that you maintain the synchrony of the previous chains. Do this matching up the chains of the previous row.

With the already gathered knowledge of making a single crochet stitch, you will need to adopt it in the making. You will need to make it in the first stitch and each of the remaining stitches of the previous chain's rows. You can recur this step until you achieve the maximum length that you desire. To make a great finishing, you need to make various cuts.

To crochet effectively, there are several steps that you need to adopt. For instance:

Step 1

Since you are crocheting with your right hand, let your right hand commence the yarn. This is making sure that your yarn is well placed on the fingers of your right hand. The end of the yarn ought to be firmly placed between the grips of your thumb. With this, you have achieved a fully functional right hand. The yarn ought to be under your fingertips and your fingers in a manner that it crosses.

Step 2

The thread that you are using ought to be placed in the middle of your right hand and forefinger in a manner that it forms a circle. After this has been achieved, you need to make the end a loop of yarn by the use of a ball end yarn that is pulled up the passing in between the circle that is formed up from the loop.

Step 3

With the knot at hand, you need to shift your focus to the hook pushing it through the topmost part of the loop. When you pull the minor end of the yarn, you will find that you have tightened the loop. As a result, you will have to come up with a slip knot.

Step 4

This is the stage where you put everything that was in your hand down on the table. Make sure that the yarn and the ball are distinct distant away from each other. With this at rest, you have the tension that you ought to deliver. This means that your stitches ought to be good and even. Using your thumb, hold the knot that has formed below the hook in a manner suggesting that you are pinching it. After you have achieved this, raise your forefinger slowly to create tension and commence the process of crocheting. Using the pencil wave pick up the crochet with the aid of your left hand, and when you have achieved this, you are ready to commence the process of crocheting.

Step 5

After you have achieved this, the hook is now facing to the right. Insert the hook downwards and make sure that your yarn over. The yarning takes place in between your finger and the hook. When this is set, you ought to hold the yarn by the use of the hook and make sure that you pull it upwards, passing inside the slip knot loop that was already inexistent on the hook. After you have achieved this, it is safe to say that you have occasioned a chain stitch. As we have earlier seen, the denotation of a chain stitch is the manner of ch. You can repeat this as many times as possible to achieve a chain.

Step 6

At this stage, you are in a position to decode the turn work slip stitch. This type of stitch is achieved when you insert the hook through the topmost part of the loop that belongs to the 2nd chain. After you have achieved this, the yarn ought to be drawn loop on the hook and the chain. This in place, you ought to make sure that the hook goes on top of the following chain, this in place you are now in a position to pull the yarn loop through the chain and the loop that has already formed on the hook. This process needs to be done repetitively until you achieve many slip-stitches.

Step 7

At this stage, you are in a position to engage in single crochet. To achieve single crochet, you need to make sure that your work is turned upside down. Make sure that the hook goes into the top loop of the final slip-stitch that was made. After you have achieved this, you're in a position to pull up a loop that should run through the slip-stitch, which was already inexistent. With this in place, you can now see to it that you pull the 2nd loop that runs past the 2 loops that have already formed on the hook. You will need to do this repetitively until you achieve what you desire.

Step 8

At this stage, you are in a position to engage in the formation of what is more like the previous stage. This stage involves the formation of double crochet. To arrive at this effect, you will need to engage in the following. The hook's movement ought to be one that is like a swing. This swing should move from the right all the way down and up in the direction of the yarn that is on the right. The last point where you worked your crochet should be the beginning point s you ought to take the hook into the last hoop that was worked on.

When you pull up the loop, this will result in 3 loops forming on the hook. With these 3 loops in place, you are now in a position to pull up another loop that passes inside 2 loops that may have formed on the hook. Make sure that you have pulled through a novel loop that originates from the previous 2 loops. When you have achieved this, it is safe to say that you have made double crochet.

Step 9

A basic understanding of various knots is possible when seeking to engage in crocheting. Crocheting may be looked at as a subtle adventure, but in the real sense, it is just the way you play with various patterns to affect something that pleases the eye. As we have already gathered, crocheting involves the process of changing between the variations of the patterns. The mastery of various patterns of crocheting is achieved through the repetitive process of doing this.

It is key to note that a large number of people can make themselves aware of crocheting just by themselves. Despite this fact, these people still have to employ the use of various aids, not limited to photos and tutorials, to achieve this. When seeking help about crocheting, you have a diverse basis on which you can draw from aid. One should not limit when seeking to crochet as the patterns that exist are a lot, and thus one can choose to settle on that that can be pleasing.

Chapter 4: How to Work Crochet for Left-Handed People

Some of the left-hand craftsmen who started to crochet years ago had to learn through their normal approach the art "backward," as they learned from only a right hand crocheted. That is no longer needed nowadays. Left-handed crochet is a reflection of right-hand crochet. The crocheted on the left keeps the crochet hook in his left pocket, and also the yarn in the right.

It implies row one has been incorporated into the base chain while you are working rows starting from the left side and heading toward the right. As a left-hander, that should feel fairly normal to you. This also means you'll crochet in the clockwise direction while you're working in circles, rather than the counter-clockwise way that righties work.

For a left-handed crotchetier, you would need to hold the crochet hook in your left hand and the yarn in the right hand. While most of the crochet tutorials are written for right-handers, left-handers can follow the same instructions but in the opposite direction. This also means that when left-handers work in rows, the first row will be worked into the foundation chain beginning from the left side and ending at the right.

As a left-hander, this is natural. When working with rounds, you will be crocheting clockwise compared to right-handers who will work counter-clockwise.

How to Crochet Chain Left-Handed

1. Start with a slip knot.

2. Yarn over. Remember that you must scoop the yarn in the clockwise direction from your hook to grab the yarn each time you "yarn over" into your crochet work.

3. Pull hook via the loop. Here you scoop the yarn in the clockwise direction.

4. Repeat steps 2 and 3; each repetition will be equal to one chain.

How to Single Crochet Left-Handed

1. Crochet any length of the base chain.

2. Insert the hook into the 2nd chain. The hook stays held into your left hand, the chain stretches to the right and the key is put in the 2nd chain on the right side of the key. So you have 2 stitches above the hook and 1 stitch below.

3. Yarn over.

4. Pull from the loop. At the end of this phase, you'll see 2 loops on your line.

5. Yarn over.

6. Draw those 2 hook loops. It's the very first **sc**.

7. Insert a hook then follow steps 3–6 in the next row.

8. Repeat step 7 along the row.

How to Double Crochet Left-Handed

1. Crochet a base chain of the length of your own choice.

2. Yarn over.

3. From hook, insert hook into the 4th chain. That is the 4th chain to that of the right that works from left to right.

4. Yarn over.

5. Draw via the loop. At the end of such a process, you'll see 3 loops about your hook.

6. Draw via the first 2 of the 3 loops onto the hook and yarn over.

7. Yarn over and pull the hook via the 2 loops. Your first double crochet has been accomplished.

8. Yarn over and put the hook into the next stitch and after that repeat steps 4–7 for the next stitch.

9. Repeat step 8 across row.

10. Turn work. Chain 3 for turning chain.

11. Yarn over and insert hook into next stitch.

How to Adapt Patterns to Left-Handed Crochet

Rest assured, if you think there aren't enough left-handed crochet patterns we have a simple solution for you. Just about any straightforward crochet pattern can be followed the way it is written. All left-handed crotchetier need to do is reverse the direction that they are working in.

However, some patterns need to be reversed properly so that they work the same way they do in their original form. In tapestry crochet for example and most crochets that require colorwork, you will need to reverse the pattern.

Otherwise, you will end up with a reversed image that looks backward. For instance, words could end up spelled backward.

If a right-handed crocheted worked the pattern with odd rows from right to left, the left-handed crocheted would need to work on them from right to left.

Chapter 5: How to Read Stitch Patterns

You'll find stitch patterns written in 2 different ways. The first is the most typical and will be found in vintage patterns, as well as many modern American and British patterns. This is a fully written out stitch pattern, using typical and traditional stitch notation. Below, you'll find a list of common abbreviations, and a few notes about translation issues, as well as a sample pattern and a breakdown of what it means.

Some modern designers in the West, as well as Japanese crochet patterns, do not rely upon written out notation but on a graphic representation of crochet stitches. These look nothing at all like craft charts you might have used, like those for cross-stitching or knitting. They are, in fact, rather pictorial with picture symbols written out for each round or row. Once you're used to reading crochet charts, you'll find you can do so with relative ease.

- Charts are much more commonly used for doilies or shawls, rather than simple projects like a hat or afghan.

- Charts are rarely used for repeated stitch patterns but can be.

Written crochet patterns are still the most common in America and Britain. They are relatively easy to use and pattern notation is largely standardized.

Which of these are the most common? For crochets, they're fairly simple: you, chi, sc, had, dc, tic. Nearly all crochet patterns are made up of these basic stitches, put together in different ways.

Most patterns also include a key explaining specific abbreviations. You may find this especially helpful if the pattern includes particular stitch patterns or combinations or if you've not crocheted for some time.

Let's look at a simple shell stitch pattern. This pattern can be used for a variety of different projects, making a pretty and feminine garment or blanket. It's relatively quick to work and easily memorized.

- Make a chain of any length desired, plus 3 stitches for turning.

- Row 1: Make 5 dc in the 3rd sty from the end, * skip 2 chi, make 1 SC in next stitch, skip 2 and make 5 dc in next stitch. *

- Row 2: Ch. 3, and turn. Work 4 dc into SC * 1 SC into 3rd dc of the previous row, 5 dc into SC of the previous row. Repeat from * across row.

- Repeat Row 2 to the desired length.

Let's take a longer look at this in a written-out form:

- **Row 1:** Make 5 double crochet stitches in the 3rd stitch from the end of the chain. *Skip 2 chains, make one single crochet in the next stitch, skip 2 chains and make 5 double crochet stitches in the next stitch. *

- **Row 2:** Chain 3 and turn. Work 4 double crochet into single crochet. Work one single crochet into 3rd double crochet of the previous row, 5 double crochet into the single crochet of the previous row. Repeat from * to end.

- With just a little practice, the abbreviations will become 2nd nature.

Do note: If you're an American and using a British pattern or you're British and using an American pattern, there's a bit of a quirk between the 2 languages.

Do you see the difference? The U.K. doesn't use the term single crochet; single crochet is called a double, and double crochet is called a treble. The treble crochet is called a double treble.

The key above illustrates crochet chart symbols. The symbols themselves are universal but do notice that the language refers to American crochet notation and work the stitches accordingly.

- **Round 1:** Ch 16, join with a sly St.

- **Round 2:** Ch 3, work one dc in the 1st chain of the previous rnd. *work one dc in next stitch, 2 dc in next around* join with a sly St. (24)

- **Round 3:** Ch 3, ski 1 dc, Sc in next, *chi 3, ski 1 dc, Sc in next* join with a sly St.

- **Round 4:** Ch 3, *1 dc in first Sc, ski 1 chi, *10 dc in 2nd chi stitch, ski 1 chi, 1 Sc in Sc* to last chi 3 loops. 9 dc in the 2nd chi sty, sly sty to join to the 3rd ch in initial ch 3.

- **Round 5:** Sc in the 6th dc of last dc cluster, ch 5, dc in sc of prep round, ch5, *sc in the 6th dc of the cluster, ch10, dc in Sc of prep round, chi 5, dc in Sc of prep round, ch5* join with a sly sty.

- **Round 6:** Working backward to reverse direction, slip stitch in the first 5 chi stitches to the left of your hook. This returns you to the corner of your work. Ch 8, Sc in the 3rd chi of chi 5 of the previous round. *Ch 5 Sc in the 3rd chi of chi 5 of the previous round. Ch5, dc 3 in the 6th ch of ch 10 of prep round, chi 3, dc3 in same space*. On the last repeat, dc 2, using the first 3 chains of initial chain 8 to make the 3rd dc. Join with sly sty at 3rd chain.

• **Round 7:** Working backward again, sly st in first 5 stitches to reach the corner of your work. Ch 8, Sc in the 3rd chi of chi 5 of the previous round. *Ch 5 sc in the 3rd ch of ch 5 of the previous round. Ch5, sc in the 3rd ch of ch 5 of prev round, dc 3 in 6th ch of ch 10 of prev round, ch 3, dc3 in same space*. On the last repeat, dc 2, using the first 3 chains of initial chain 8 to make the 3rd dc. Join with sl st at the 3rd chain.

• **Round 8:** Working backward again, sl st in first 5 stitches to reach the corner of your work. Ch 8, sc in the 3rd ch of ch 5 of the previous round. *Ch 5 sc in the 3rd ch of ch 5 of the previous round. Ch5, sc in the 3rd ch of ch 5 of prev round, Ch5, sc in the 3rd ch of ch 5 of prev round, dc 3 in the 6th ch of ch 10 of prev round, ch 3, dc3 in same space*. On the last repeat, dc 2, using the first 3 chains of initial chain 8 to make the 3rd dc. Join with sl st at the 3rd chain.

Note: Rounds 6, 7, and 8 are nearly identical, with the addition of one more ch5 loop per side in each round.

As you can see, that's a very cumbersome pattern written out. It's much easier to follow and understand working from a pictorial chart. This is the benefit of charts for complex and lacy work. If you'd like, you can even make your charts, either by hand or using online charting software.

Chapter 6: Easy Patterns for Beginners to Get You Started

Slip Knot

Knowing how to create the slip knot is the 1st step towards developing your crocheting ability. The slip knot is the basis of most crochet patterns, and therefore, you will need to properly master this so that you can build your ability to pick on other trends then.

So, you will begin with laying the thread on a flat surface, then looping once over itself. Here, you will have the tail yarn and working yarn. Tail yarn will be the part that is on the right side, while the working yarn is the end of the string on the left, which is pretty much how crochet begins.

Then, loop over with your thread, so that the rear part of the wool comes over the one you are working with. Then, once you have done this, run the end of the wool over where they cross and move the loop beneath the working wool.

After this, insert the crochet hook through the right side to the left, passing it over the wool you are working with then through the cross you have made. Then tighten the wool over the hoop. Pull lightly on both ends to tighten it. Congratulations, you've just made your first knot.

The Foundation Chain

Here you hold the hook with the back end downwards while you hold the tail of the string on your other hand, using the finger grip that you are comfortable with using. The key is that you maintain it well such that it will be easy for you to make the loops without disrupting the movement of the crochet shaft.

Then move it over, with the wool coming to the left side of the hook, then move it to the left side of the first knot. Then, move the working thread through the slip knot, and you will have one loop on the hook and another underneath it. This is your first chain.

Do this over and over depending on the number of chains that you want to create. So say you want to create 12 strings, then you will repeat this process over and over 12 times. Do this repeatedly until you can comfortably move the crochet through the working yarn, slip knot, and loops with ease and comfort.

Single Crochet (sc)

This comes as the 3rd step in making your crochet. Once you have your chain, you will have them looped into each other with v shapes, with the first end of it on the right side. Put your hook through the right side of the 2nd V in the chain.

When you have done this, move over the working yarn, pulling it to the top side of the crochet hook.

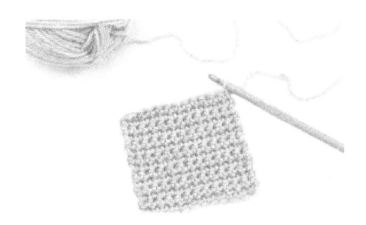

Then move the working yarn through the V, bringing the moving wool through the procession you have woven, which will then create 2 running folds on the hook shaft. Then move it over once more, moving the working yarn back through the underside of the hook, passing it through the 2 loops you have when you do this. You will have one knot on the crochet hook. This is the first crochet that you have made.

To do this, you will need to understand that you will need always to be using the working yarn to make all the loops. That is why it is called the working yarn, after all. Be keen to keep it long then, as you do not want to run out of thread midway through your loop, bringing to a sad end the beautiful artistry that was taking shape.

Once you have completed your first single crochet, then repeat the process through each of the rows of the foundation chain and keep in mind that you will continue using the 2nd V-shaped loops, as this will ensure that you do not have significant unsightly gaps in your knitting.

You will repeat this process for as long as you need, depending on the size of what you are knitting. Then, you move to a third party.

The Turning Chain

To begin with your turning chain, first, you will need to flip over the foundation chain, but still maintaining the basic crochet rule—you work from right to left. When you flip it over, this will mean that you will have reversed it, with what was on the left now on the right, and vice versa.

Then, begin to create a chain through the single crochet so that you create your first stitch.

Double Crochet (dc)

Here, you will yarn over then pull the hook into the 4th chain. Then pull through the string so that you now have 3 loops running through your hook. Then yarn over again and bring the hook through 2 of the circles, leaving the one at the end. So it again, and you have created 1 double crochet. You will then create 3 chains at the end to bring up a turning chain that will be the basis of the first double crochet in the new chain that you will form.

So, what patterns can you make from this?

Crochet Socks

Crochet socks are other easy designs that you will find easier to do when you are a beginner.

According to Clara Parkes, the best yarns for socks are those that are elastic, meaning that they will need to stretch when you dip your foot into it, then wrap around the foot comfortably and warmly once you have worn it.

You will use your basic crochet techniques when you do this, while you will need additional experience to make more complex socks like ankle-high socks and those with frilled edges or fancy patterns.

However, if you want simple, ankle-length socks, here you will need to alternate between the single crochet and double crochet. You will alternate between these 2, lapping them over each other as you move through the foundation's chains, leaving the fabric closely-knit. This is what we call the seed stitch crochet.

So, you being with your foundation chain and then flip it over and begin to work on the turning chain, then make the first stitch, which will work as your first double crochet in the 1st row. Then, start to alternate between the dc and sc. Once you make your first dc, then, make the sc after that, then the dc, sc as you progress. Then make these stitches across the rows. When you start with a dc, you will then end the row with sc.

Once you finish, turn it over and begin working on the turning chain. But since you will have flipped over the wool, you will be working in reverse, your dc going above sc and your sc going above dc.

To continue creating the rows that you need, repeat the process from the moment when you made your first dc. You will repeat this process depending on how long you want the socks to be, though as a beginner, you should probably make it as short as possible as you work on your hand movements and ironing out the problems that may arise when you make a mistake.

Crochet Seat Covers

You will find these in many homes and cars, providing the room with an antique, authentic, and comforting feel. And the thing about these is that the patterns are relatively easy to follow, with the size and design also mainly depending on how you want it. But you will want to keep it straight if you're going to create extensive material.

Once you have done your slip knot and created your foundation chain, then make 4 stitches and 2 rows. Then, in the first round, create 8 single crochet stitches then make 2 sc stitches in each stitch.

In this, as with the socks, you will alternate between dc and sc. Once you create the 2 first rows, create another chain. Then, on the 1st row, the 4th chain from the hook, make dc through until the end of the row. Then, on the 2nd chain, on the 2nd row, make double crochet until the end. Repeat this on the 3rd row, 3rd chain. Once you have finished these, then close the terms. At this point, you will have a square granny design, and you will then work from here through with additional rows and chains depending on how long you want it to be and how much you want it to cover the seat.

However, if you want to add on color and make it larger, create additional rows and chains using wool from the color that you want to infuse to the cover.

Square Blanket

This is one other straightforward pattern that you can learn. This one will also turn out great with just one color, though you will then have to put a lot of time into it so that you can achieve the thickness and size that you want.

Using the basis of the granny square, make your foundation chain then create 3 more. Begin to make double crochets then, then loop them to create double stitches. After this, then connect these 2 double stitches through the 3rd chain. After this, create another 3 dc but with the dc going into the foundation of the 1st round.

Go through this step until you get to the size that you desire. Or extra thickness, you could use the technique of socks and use alternating dc and sc to create additional loops and knots to the width that you desire.

Alternatively, you can still use this basis to create a table cover, but then you will not need to make it substantial and thick as you would have with a blanket.

Crochet Sweater for Beginners

The basis of making the sweater is starting from how you would make the granny square. Make 2 of such rectangles, with the size depending on who you are making it. Use dc for making the rectangle that you will make the front so that it is one solid piece with minimal gaps. You could also use this for the back, or use sc to leave a see-through back for extra aesthetics.

So, create 9 chains, with 2 rows. Here, make an sc through the 2nd chain from the hook. Make a total of 8 sc. In the 2nd row, stitch across the first chain, back loops only (blo). Then repeat this with the 2nd row to row 65 or above, depending on the size to fit on the waist, chest, and hips. Note that you will need the rows to be odd numbers.

Then move to the 1st row, and in the 1st chain, turn it and make sc across the band, with one running across each row, down to the number of rows that you have for the sweater and the region it fits.

In the 2nd row, loop through the 3rd chain, turn and make double crochet across all rows. In the 3rd row, repeat the 2nd process. Through the 4th row through to the 7th, make the stitches on the chain lose.

Then in the 8th row, go through the 3rd chain, turn it and make a double crochet in each dc and chain space so that you create a close-knit loop through each row until the end. In the 9th row, the 3rd chain, make dc across all rows until the end. Use this technique for the back rectangle, but then you will use sc and dc alternately depending on if you want the gaps or not.

Chapter 7: Simple Afghan Patterns

Basic Yo-Yo Pattern Afghan

A yo-yo afghan gives a unique circular pattern. It's fun and very different so will leave you with a product to be proud of! The pattern is worked in rounds.

Hook: I-9.

Yarn: 1 skein of worsted weight yarn (approx. 62" of yarn needed).

Other materials: Tapestry needle.

Gauge swatch: 24 stitches = 4 inches.

Pattern instructions:

Create a slip knot and chain 4 stitches. Join these with a slip stitch in the first chain to create a ring.

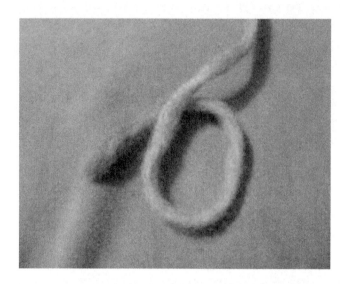

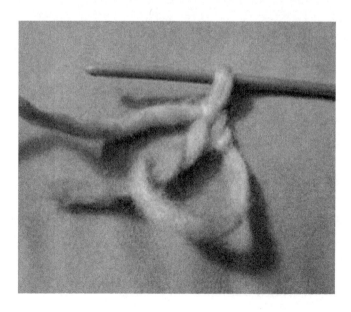

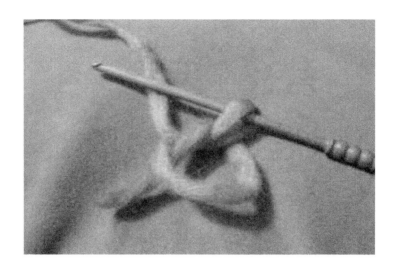

Round 1:

Chain 3 as the first double crochet, work 11 more double crochet stitches in the ring and fasten off.

Flat braid joins method:

1st yo-yo:

1. Join with a single crochet in any double crochet.

2. Chain 3, then single crochet in the next double crochet 11 times.

3. Join with a slip stitch in the first single crochet.

4. Fasten off.

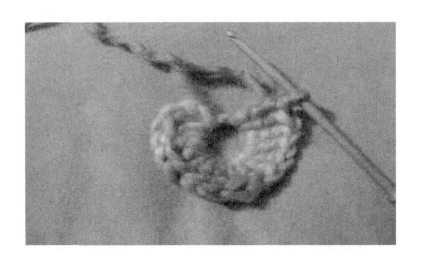

2nd yo-yo:

1. Join with a single crochet in one of the double crochet stitches.

2. Chain 3, then single crochet in the double crochet 9 times.

3. Chain 1.

4. Single crochet (inserting the hook from the bottom) in any chain-3 space on the first yo-yo.

5. Chain 1, then single crochet in the next double crochet on the 2nd yo-yo.

6. Chain 1, then single crochet in the next chain- 3 space on the 1st yo-yo.

7. Chain 1, then single crochet in the next double crochet on the 2nd yo-yo.

8. Chain 3, then join with a slip stitch in the first single crochet on the 2nd yo-yo.

9. Fasten off.

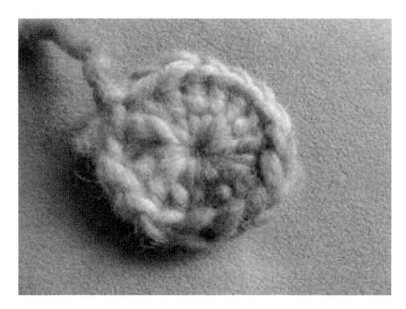

3rd yo-yo:

Join in loops 1 and 2 as done with the 2nd yo-yo.

Easy Openwork Crochet Pattern

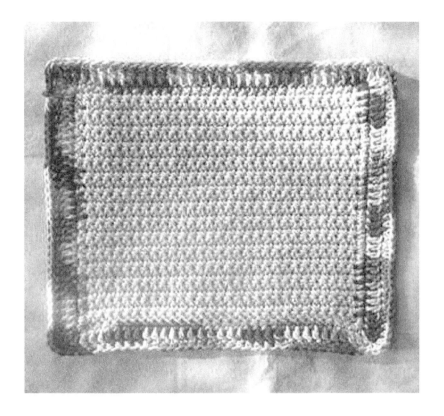

This pattern produces a pretty afghan that can be matched with any decor. It can be a perfect gift for any occasion.

Blanket Size: 44"x54"

Hook: K-10.

Yarn: 6 skeins (Lions Brand Homespun Sierra is preferred).

Other materials: Tapestry needle.

Gauge size: 10 sts = 10 cm, 8 rows = 13 cm.

Pattern instructions:

Foundation row:

Working on the right side, single crochet in the 2nd chain from the hook. Chain across until you've made 101 stitches. Turn your work.

Row 1:

1. Chain 4 stitches, then treble crochet in the next stitch.

2. Chain 2, miss out on the next stitch, then work 1 half double crochet, 1 double crochet, 3 single crochet stitches, chain 2, miss a stitch, 1 double crochet, and 1 half-double crochet—repeat until the last 2 stitches.

3. Treble crochet in the last 2 single crochet stitches.

4. Turn your work.

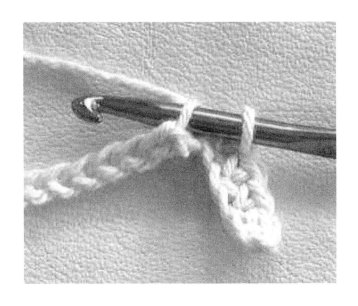

Row 2:

1. Chain 1 and single crochet in the first 2 treble crochet stitches.

2. *2 single crochet in the next chain, 2 spaces, single crochet in the next, 3 single crochet stitches, 2 single crochet in chain, 2 spaces.*

3. Single crochet in 3 treble crochet stitches.

4. Repeat from *to.*

5. Single crochet in the last 2 treble crochet stitches.

6. Turn your work.

Row 3:

1. Chain 3 stitches, double crochet in each remaining single crochet across.

Row 4:

1. Chain 1, single crochet in first 2 double crochet stitches.

2. Half-double crochet in the next double crochet stitch.

3. Double crochet in the next double crochet stitch.

4. Treble crochet in the next 3 stitches.

5. Repeat rows 1–4 then repeat rows 1–2 once more.

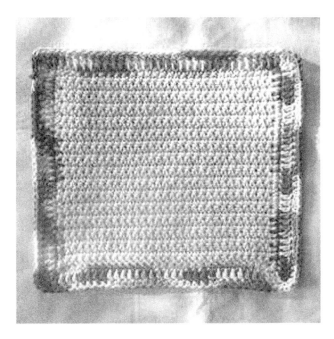

Checkerboard Stitch Afghan

The checkerboard stitch afghan is suitable for those cool summer evenings. It may not produce the warmest product, but it looks amazing.

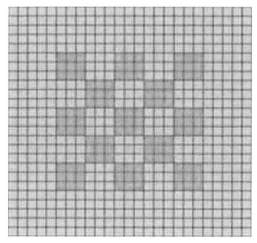

Blanket Size: 46"x63".

Hook: F-5.

Yarn: 3 skeins of worsted weight yarn.

Other materials: Tapestry needle.

Gauge size: 15 stitches=4-inches.

Pattern Instructions:

Step 1: Make a slip knot and chain 101 stitches. Double crochet in the 3rd stitch from the hook, then again in the next stitch.

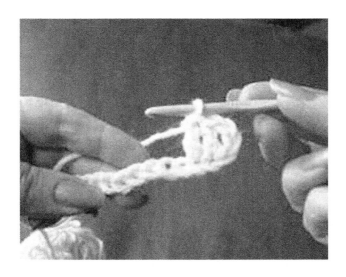

Step 2: Chain 3, miss out on the next 3 stitches.

Step 3: Double crochet in each of the next 3 stitches.

Step 4: Repeat steps 2 and 3 across the row. Be sure to finish double crochet in the last stitch.

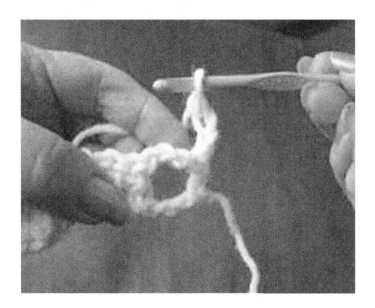

Step 5: Chain 3 and turn.

Step 6: Create 2 double crochet stitches in the chain-3 space of the former row. Chain 3 obtains the place of the first double crochet.

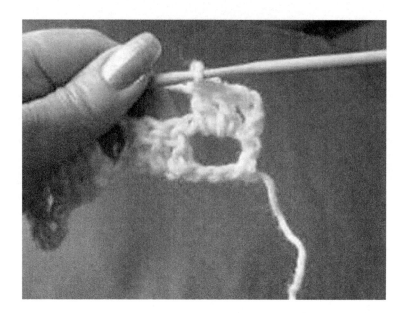

Step 7: Chain 3 stitches and 3 double crochet in the chain-3 space of the earlier row.

Step 8: Repeat step 6 across the row.

Step 9: Repeat all the above steps until the afghan is your desired length.

Step 10: Finish off.

Easy Ripple Afghan

The ripple design looks great in a variety of colors and will look impressive for a gift or in your own home.

Blanket Size: 40"x60"

Hook: I-9.

Yarn: Worsted weight yarn in a variety of colors.

Other materials: Tapestry needle, scissors.

Gauge size: 4 stitches = 1 inch.

Pattern instructions:

Make a slip knot and chain 178 stitches.

Row 1:

1. Double crochet in the 3rd chain from the hook.

2. Double crochet in the next 6 chains.

3. Work 3 double crochet stitches in the next chain.

4. Double crochet in the next 6 chains.

5. Work a 3 stitch decrease in the next 3 chains.

6. Double crochet in the next 6 chains.

7. Work 3 double crochet stitches in the next chain.

8. Double crochet in the next 6 chains.

9. Repeat above 4 across the row.

10. Finish by working a 2 stitch decrease in the last 2 chains.

11. Chain 2 and turn.

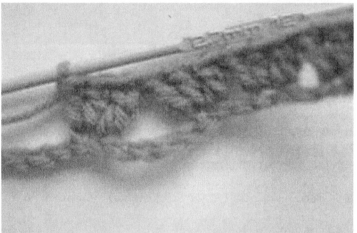

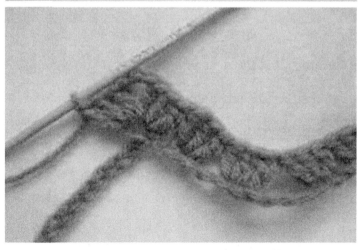

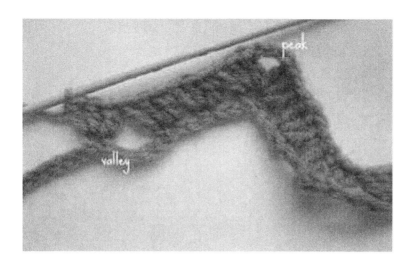

Row 2:

1. Skip the first stitch.

2. Double crochet in the next 7 stitches.

3. Work 3 double crochet stitches in the next double crochet.

4. Double crochet in the next double crochet stitches.

5. Work a 3 stitch decrease in the next 3 chains.

6. Double crochet in the next 6 chains.

7. Work 3 double crochet stitches in the next chain.

8. Double crochet in the next 6 chains.

9. Repeat above 4 across the row.

10. Finish by working a 2 stitch decrease in the last 2 chains.

11. Chain 2 and turn.

12. Repeat row 2 until the afghan is the desired length, changing colors as you like, then fasten off.

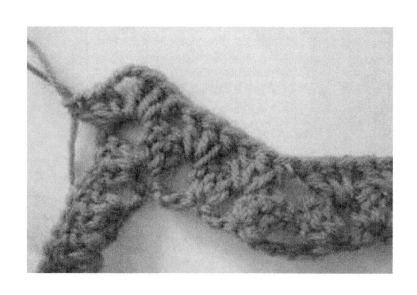

Chapter 8: Fun Crochet Patterns

As a beginner, finding easy and fun patterns for your first few projects is crucial for starting your crochet journey. This will help you get the hang of reading patterns, improve hand-eye coordination between the yarn, the hook, and the stitches, and most importantly, it will allow you to build enough confidence to get through the entire project. Once you have finished it, you may move on to more advanced patterns in due time. Whether you are crocheting as a hobby, or wish to make Christmas gifts for everybody, the patterns described are great for beginners and are an excellent way to kickstart your crocheting journey.

Simple Bow

Are you itching to start a quick and easy project? Are you looking for useful crochet projects that will make use of those scrap yarns? I've got you covered! The next few pages are filled with small projects like a coin purse, a bow, motifs, and more.

This project will surely add character and personalized touch to any hair tie, headband, shirt, beanie, denim jacket, or present.

Note: This works well with any kind of yarn, just make sure you use the appropriate hook according to the yarn's thickness.

1st Row

1. Make 12 chains. 2nd to 22nd Row.

2. Make 12 dc on top of the previous row.

How to assemble:

1. Sew both the 1st and 22nd rows together.

2. Lay it flat with the seam in the middle.

3. Pinch the middle with your thumb and index finger and loop the remaining yarn around the strip to form a bow.

4. Secure the yarn at the pack of the bow, fasten in place, and tuck off the ends.

Crochet Scrunchie

This lovely, personalized scrunchie will be a great gift for your female friends and family members.

Note: This works well with any kind of yarn, just make sure you use the appropriate hook according to the yarn's thickness. Here, I suggest a light cotton 3-ply thread.

1st round:

1. Make a slip knot into the ponytail band. Work your 1st sc.

2. Make 3 chains, then sc into the band.

3. Repeat step 2 until you've covered the entire band. Allow them to overlap each other to hide the band completely.

4. When completely covered, slip stitch into your 1st stitch.

2nd row:

1. SC into the 1st chain space you come across.

2. Chain 3 and SC into the chain space of 3.

3. Repeat step 2 until you've gone through each chain space of 3.

4. Slip stitch into your 1st stitch.

3rd round:

1. Slipstitch into the nearest chain space and make chain 3. Make 5 dc into the same chain space, then SC into the next chain space.

2. Make 6 dc into the next chain space, and then 1 SC into the next chain space.

3. Repeat step 2 until you've reached your 1st stitch for this round. Fasten it off and tuck in ends.

Rainbow Fold-Over Coin Purse

Easy, simple, and eye-catching—talk about aesthetics and functionality. Have fun making this in rainbow shades, gradient shades, or alternate between your favorite colors.

Note: This works well with any kind of yarn, just make sure you use the appropriate hook according to the yarn's thickness.

1st round:

1. Make a Magic Ring.

2. Make 3 Chains and 12 dc into the Magic Ring.

3. Slip stitch into the 1st stitch you made and fasten off. You should have 13 stitches in total.

2nd round:

Change yarn color.

1. Make a dc into one of the stitches from the previous row. Pass in a 2nd dc into the same stitch.

2. Finish this round by making 2 dc in each stitch from the previous round.

3. Slip stitch into the 1st stitch you made and fasten off. You should have 26 dc in total.

3rd round:

Change yarn color.

1. Start with 1 dc into any stitch from the previous round.

2. In the next stitch, make 2 dc into the same stitch, and make 1 dc in the next stitch.

3. Repeat step 2 until you finish this round, alternating between 2 dc and 1 dc.

4. Slip stitch into your 1st stitch and fasten off. You should have 39 dc.

4th round:

Change yarn color.

1. Make 2 dc in 2 separate stitches.

2. Make 2 dc into 1 stitch.

3. Repeat steps 1 and 2 until you finish this round, alternating between 2 dc in 2 separate stitches and 1 2 dc in the same stitch.

4. Slip stitch into the 1st stitch you made and fasten off. You should have 52 dc.

5th round:

Change yarn color.

1. In this round, make 3 dc in 3 separate stitches, and stitch in 2 dc into the 4th stitch.

2. Keep alternating between 3 dc in 3 separate stitches, and stitch in 2 dc into the 4th stitch.

3. Slipstitch into the 1st stitch you made and fasten off. You should have 65 dc.

6th round:

Change yarn color.

1. In this round, make 4 dc in 3 separate stitches, and stitch in 2 dc into the 5th stitch.

2. Keep alternating between 4 dc in 3 separate stitches, and stitch in 2 dc into the 5th stitch.

3. Slipstitch into the first stitch you made and fasten off. You should have 78 dc.

7th round:

Change yarn color.

1. In this round, make 5 dc in 3 separate stitches, and stitch in 2 dc into the 6th stitch.

2. Keep alternating between 5 dc in 3 separate stitches, and stitch in 2 dc into the 6th stitch.

3. Slipstitch into the first stitch you made and fasten off. You should have 91 dc.

How to assemble:

1. With a needle and thread, sew in a zipper on half of the circle.

2. Fold over, and sew in the other half onto the other side of the zipper.

3. Embellish with beads and sequins or leave as is.

Tube Pencil Case

We all could use a cute pencil case! Try making this convenient and easy-to-fashion pencil case for yourself or a loved one.

Note: This works well with any kind of yarn, just make sure you use the appropriate hook according to the yarn's thickness.

You will need:

- Needle.

- Button.

We will be working around this project in a spiral, so no need to make a slip stitch after every round.

1st Round:

1. Make a Magic Ring.

2. Make 6 SCs into the Magic Ring.

2nd round:

Make 2 SCs in each stitch from the previous round. You should have 12 SCs in total.

3rd round:

1. Make 2 SCs in one stitch, then follow up with 2 SCs in 2 stitches.

2. Repeat step 1 until you finish this round. You should have a total of 18 SCs.

4th round:

1. SC the back loop only of each stitch from the previous round, maintaining 18 SCs throughout each round. Repeat this step until you get to your desired length.

Closure Flap

1ˢᵗ Row:

1. Chain 1 and then turn your work over.

2. Make 7 SCs.

2ⁿᵈ–5ᵗʰ row:

Repeat 1ˢᵗ row.

6ᵗʰ row:

1. Chain 1 then turn your work over.

2. Make 2 SCs into the next 2 stitches, then Chain 3, skip 3 stitches, and finally SC into the last 2 stitches.

7ᵗʰ row:

1. Make 1 Chain and SC through all 7 stitches from the previous row.

2. Now slowly keep making SCs around the flap and the rim of the pencil case to make it look neat. Slip stitch, fasten off and tuck in the ends.

3. Position the button and sew in place. Fasten off and tuck in the ends.

African Flower Hexagon

This is one of the most versatile patches you will find in the history of crochet. If you join them together, you can create unique things like stuffed animals, blankets, pillowcases, balls, purses, and so much more. The trick to it is to use random colors to make them brighter and eye-catching. This is a good way to make use of scrap yarns.

The pattern is pretty straightforward and easy to do. Connecting it and experimenting with ideas is what will creativity and style.

Note: This works well with any kind of yarn, just make sure you use the appropriate hook according to the yarn's thickness.

1st row:

1. Start with a Magic Ring.

2. Chain 3 (this will be considered as your 1st dc) and next to it, make a dc, and then a chain.

3. Make 5 more sets of 2 dc and 1 chain stitch. You will end up with 6 in total.

4. After your last chain, slip stitch into your first dc (the 3 Chains).

2nd row:

This will be a good time to change colors.

1. Fasten off into the 1st chain to your left.

2. This row will consist of chain-centered fan stitches. Having said that, chain 3, dc into the chain space, chain 1, 2 dc into the same chain space. Continue until you have 6 of these around your circle. One set for each chain from the previous row.

3. End this row by slip stitching into your first stitch.

3rd row:

1. Fasten off into the 1st chain to your left.

2. Now create a full fan of 7 dc. 1st fan should consist of 3 chains and 6 dc. Make 6 of these, 1 set for each Chain from the previous row.

3. And like before, end this row with a slip stitch to your first stitch.

4th row:

This will be a good time to change colors again.

1. This row will consist of SCs. Fasten off into the 2nd dc from the previous row.

2. Start making your SCs around the previous row's dc.

3. When you reach where the fans of the previous row meet, make a long stitch, going through all the way to where the fans from the 2nd row meet.

4. Continue your SCs around the fans, do not forget to make a long stitch where the fans meet.

5. When you've gone all around the flower, slip stitch into your 1st stitch.

5th row:

This is another time to change colors if you please.

1. Make SCs around the flower again, but this time, only in the back loops.

2. Take off from the last stitch you had left off, make 3 scs, and when you reach the "corner" of the hexagon (which is the 4th stitch from the previous row, in other words, the center of the "petal,") make a Chain before making another sc in the same stitch.

3. Keep making scs on the back loops of the previous row, remembering that when you reach the center stitch of the "petal" you need to make a Chain, and then make an sc again in the same loop the last stitch was in.

African Flower Pin Cushion

Are you tired of that old tomato pin cushion? Make your sewing kit bright and cheerful with this lovely project.

Note: This works well with any kind of yarn, just make sure you use the appropriate hook according to the yarn's thickness.

How to assemble:

1. Make 2 African Flower Hexagons.
2. Sew on buttons in the center of both African Flower Hexagons.
3. Sc both their edges together. Just before you're about to close the seam, stuff it with polyester filling to make it puff up.
4. Continue your sc until it's fully closed.
5. Slip stitch into your 1st stitch.
6. Fasten off and tuck the ends away.

Chapter 9: Crochet Patterns

By combining the Grundmaschenarten in groups, you can also crochet very pretty patterns. Below you will learn how to crochet shell patterns, tufts, and (flat) pimples, as well as puff and popcorn stitches.

Mussel Pattern

For this pattern, 3 or more stitches are crocheted into the same puncture site, forming a triangle that looks like a small shell. On the left and right of the shell, one usually goes over a few stitches to compensate for the increase in stitches by the shells, which turn one stitch into at least 3. Shells look best if you crochet them out of chopsticks or double sticks.

To crochet a mussel out of 3 sticks, 1 works first, where the stitch is to be placed, first a stick, to work. Then in the same puncture, place 2 more sticks. To complete the pattern and the number of stitches in the row, it can sometimes be necessary to crochet half-shells at the beginning and end of the row.

To do this, at the beginning of each turn, work 2 sticks into the corresponding puncture site. At the end of the row, place 2 sticks in the last stitch.

Tuft Stitches

Tufts are nothing but inverted shells. They consist of several stitched-together stitches; these can be fixed stitches but also double or multiple sticks. Not only do they provide a decorative pattern, but they are also often used to remove one or more stitches in a row.

The base of this tuft is spread over several stitches while their heads are gathered in a stitch. To do this, do not crochet the stitches you want to gather at first to pull the thread in one go through all loops on the needle in the last step. How to do it exactly, shows the following instructions for a tuft of 3 sticks.

1. Work the 1st stick as usual until there are only 2 loops on the needle. Do the same with the 2nd stick so that you have a total of 3 loops on the needle.

2. The 3rd stick is also crocheted up to and including the penultimate step. There are 4 loops on the needle. Now, get the thread.

3. To complete the tufting, pull the thread through all 4 loops on the needle.

Burl

Knob stitches are very distinctive and give the crochet a beautiful plastic structure. It is a group of several rods or multiple rods, which are worked in the same puncture site and then blended, making it a combination of shell and tufts. Pimples are worked in the back row.

The following shows how to crochet a knot stitch out of 5 sticks.

1. Crochet the 1st stick at the point where you want to create the knit stitch until you have only 2 loops on the needle.

2. Follow the same procedure for the following 4 rods working in the same puncture site.

3. Now, there should be a total of 6 loops on the crochet hook.

4. In the last step, pick up the thread and pull it in one go through all the loops on the needle. It is advisable to secure the knit stitch with a chain stitch (take the thread and pull it once again through the stitch on the needle) so that the stitches remain firmly together at the top and the knobby effect maintains the desired plasticity.

Colorful Pimples

It looks happy when you work the pimples in different colors. Also, you can meaningfully use small yarn remnants in this way.

To crochet a colored nub, work the last solid stitch in front of the nub in the base color until there are still 2 loops on the needle to finish the stitch with the yarn for the nub.

Then crochet the nub as described in the new color. Use the chain stitch to secure the knob; work again in the basic color, with which you then continue crocheting until the next knob.

Flat Nubs

Flat knobs are made of half-sticks and are slightly less plastic than knobs or the popcorn stitches described below. They are often used to crochet baby clothes and cuddly blankets. They are crocheted according to the same principle as the pimples.

It is important that you do not work too hard. The following example illustrates how to crochet a flat knot of 3 half rods in one go through all the loops on the needle.

It is advisable to secure the knit stitch with a chain stitch (take the thread and pull it once again through the stitch on the needle) so that the stitches remain firmly together at the top, and the knobby effect maintains the desired plasticity.

1. First, thread the thread around the needle, then insert it into the loop into which the flat knot should be placed. Get the thread.

2. Repeat this step twice so that there are finally 7 loops on the crochet hook. Then you pick the thread and pull it in one go through all the loops.

3. Finally, secure the flat knot with a warp stitch by retrieving the thread and pulling it through the loop on the crochet hook.

Popcorn Stitches

For a popcorn mesh, one work—as well as the knobs or flat knobs—a whole group of stitches in a puncture site. The stitches are not taken off together but individually terminated and bundled in a further step. They create plastic accents in even patterns and can be crocheted from fine yarn, as well as from thicker wool qualities.

1. Crochet a group of 5 rods in a single injection site when you wanted to crochet a shell. Then slightly lengthen the working loop on the needle by pulling lightly.

2. Now, pull the needle out of the working loop to put it into the debarking element (i.e., the mesh V) of the 1st stick.

3. Then, pick up the working loop and pull it through the 2nd loop on the needle (the debittering stick of the first stick). Secure the stitch with a chain stitch. Pull the thread through the loop again.

Filet or Net Pattern

For this effective but, in principle, quite simple pattern, you crochet from bars, and air meshes a grid. You can combine filled and empty boxes in such a way that geometric or floral motifs are created. A simple net pattern without "fillings" can be crocheted very fast. For example, it is good for light scarves and bandages, and if you can handle it with sturdy material works, you would have crocheted, in no time, a shopping net. If you work alternately filled and empty boxes, you can pull a cord through the stitches to close about a bag.

1. Crochet a chain of meshes first. The number of stitches for your basic chain must be divisible by 2. Also, crochet 6 more pieces of air.

2. Now, for the first box, insert into the 6th stitch of the chain of stitches as seen from the needle and work a chopstick.

3. Crochet an airlock again. For the subsequent chopsticks, pass over a stitch in the sling chain. Then, crochet one more air mesh and the next chopstick into the next, but one mesh of the basic chain work. So, continue until the end of the series.

4. Start the next row with 3 first-streaks and one streak with the next-stick link.

5. Now, work a chopstick into the scraping member of the penultimate stick of the previous row, crochet a loop of air, pass one stitch of the previous row, and work another stick into the corresponding chopsticks of the previous row. The last stitch of the row works in the 3rd link of the chain of meshes counted from below.

6. To crochet a filled box, do not join the sticks with an airlock, but crochet between the base sticks other sticks around the air mesh of the previous row. To do this, just stick in the empty box to get the thread.

7. If the box of the previous row is also filled, work the "stuffing stick" into the scraping member of the pre-row filler.

Grid Pattern

A likewise light and transparent pattern is the grid pattern, which is crocheted from air mesh and solid or warp stitches. Experimental minds vary the length of the air-chain chains to work an uneven lattice structure.

Normally, the arcs are 1/3-longer than the basic piece of the previous series. The arcs in the following instructions are 5 air mesh long, the base 3 chains.

1. Work an air chain. The number of stitches should be divisible by 4. For this crochet, add 2 air meshes.

2. Now, anchor the first bow by crocheting it into the 6th stitch of the base with a slit stitch or a sturdy stitch. Then crochet 5 loops of air, pass 3 meshes in the basic loop and anchor the bow in the 4th loop of the air.

3. The last bow of the row is attached in the last loop of the base chain.

4. Now, crochet 5 air stitches and then a single crochet stitch into the bow, then another 5 stitches, and then a single crochet stitch into the next bow. The last bow is anchored in the 3rd spiral of the 1st row.

5. Start the next series again with 5 air stitches, fasten them with a sturdy stitch in the 1st loop of air mesh, and work in the grid pattern to the end of the row. The last tight stitch back into the 3rd spiral air mesh of the front row work. Continue working until the desired height is reached.

Crochet Subjects Around an Air-Mesh Bow

In crochet instructions for flowers, for example, one often reads the instruction that a group of stitches, often chopsticks, should be worked into an air-mesh arch. For this, you do not sting into the mesh links of the chain but into the bow so that the chain of mesh is crocheted.

If you are interested in making one of these models, you can for the first time follow one of the many video tutorials, step by step, that are found online and have fun trying them.

Chapter 10: Crochet for Advanced

The shell stitch is used in many advanced crochet patterns, learning to create this stitch will add a new level to your crochet abilities. Here are a few items made with the crocheted shell stitch.

To begin your shell stitch square, ch 33, then sc in the stitch next to the hook, *skip 2 stitches then dc 5 in the next stitch*. You have now created a shell, repeat from *to* until you have completed a row.

Now skip 2 stitches and dc 3 in the last stitch, ch 1, and turn.

Sc in the first dc, then *skip the next 2 stitches and dc 5 in the next stitch. Skip the next 2 stitches and sc in the next dc*, this is a complete shell. Repeat from *to* until the row is complete.

Now skip 2 stitches and dc 3 in the last stitch, ch 1, and turn.

This is what your work should look like after you complete 3 rows the different colors are used to show the individual shell motif:

Continue making shells and rows until you reach your desired size. Your completed square should look something like this, the different colors are used to show the shells:

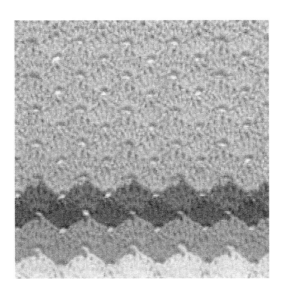

The shell stitch is used in many patterns, it is a light airy stitch, perfect for spring sweaters, and lightweight baby blankets. This stitch also looks great as a border or with a border.

Using lightweight yarns such as sport or baby weight will make your work airy and soft because the stitch is airy and open. You can combine this stitch with a border of picot trim for a soft cozy baby blanket. It works up quickly and it is very attractive done in solids or multiple colors. If you do not have a pattern for a baby blanket, just chain your first row as long as you want the blanket to be, then make rows of shell stitches until it is the length you want.

When you are finished, complete a border using the picot stitch and that's it, instant baby blanket and great shower gift.

Solomon's Knot Stitch

Solomon's knot is an openwork technique that is perfect for bathing suit cover-ups, long vests, or any other item that you want to layer. After several rows of Solomon's knot, the pattern begins to resemble a fishing net.

The size of the stitch changes depending on how long or short the loop is drawn; some patterns use 1/4-inch, 1/2-inch, or even as large as 3-inches! This is a fun stitch to add to your crochet technique repertoire; it can be added to a project for a bit of interest or flair or used to complete an entire project.

You can do Solomon's knot as small or as large as you wish. Once you get the hang of it you can create a tighter, smaller weave that is great for fashion scarves or fingerless gloves, and it even looks great as decoration over plain patterns.

Remember to keep your tension steady, this will help you create an evenly spaced stitch that will look better when the project is complete.

Solomon's Knot

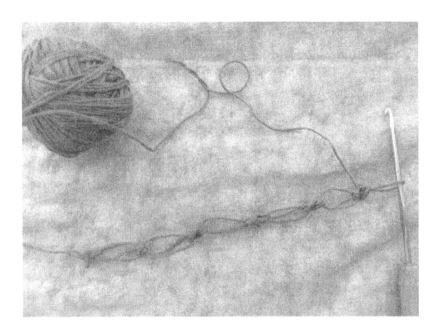

Step 1

Ch 2 then sc in the first stitch.

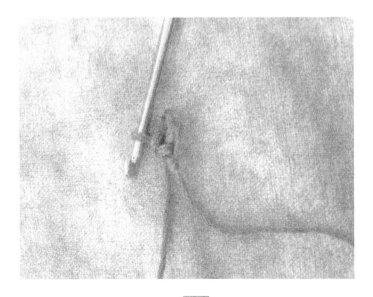

Step 2

Pull up the loop on your hook, enlarge it by tugging upward until you reach the height in the pattern; in this case, make it about 1-inch.

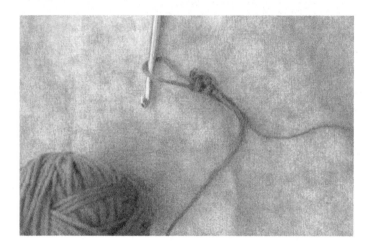

Step 3

Yo and pull through the long loop on the hook. Pull up the yarn on the hook until it is as long as the yarn in the back.

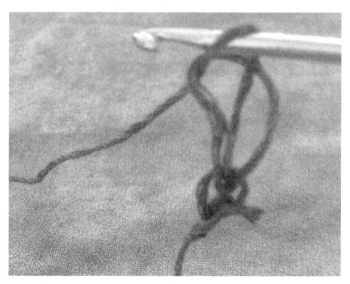

Step 4

Put your hook under the yarn in the back and yo, then pull through the first loop on the hook.

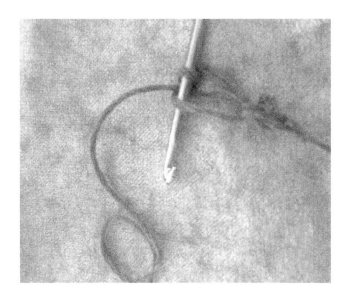

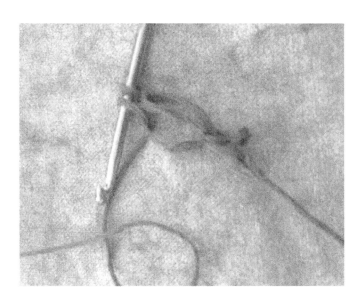

Step 5

Yo and pull through both loops on the hook.

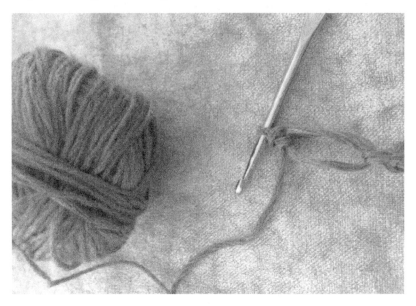

Step 6

To crochet, the next knot pulls up the last loop on your hook to make it 1-inch long and repeat steps 3 through 5.

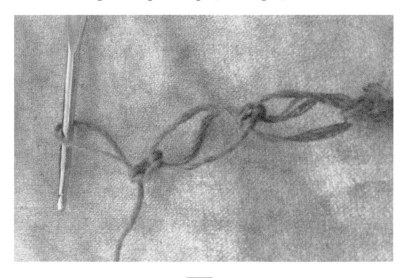

Here are a few items created using Solomon's knot stitch.

Waffles Anyone?

The waffle stitch looks like the stitches in a thermal shirt, only on a much larger scale. This stitch is great for all types of warm items. The closeness of the waffle stitch and the bulk it creates is extra warm for blankets, scarves, and other items for keeping warm. The texture is a nice touch for throw pillows and roll pillows. Here are a few items created with the waffle stitch:

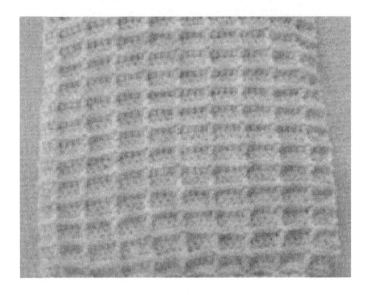

The waffle stitch is easy to do, just follow these instructions to create squares for your sampler.

Ch 30 then single crochet in each stitch across the row. Now ch 3, then dc in each stitch across the row. Now ch 3 and fpdc (same as bpdc only you insert the hook from the back to the front, the post will be in front of the hook) around the next post. Now dc in the next stitch. It should look like this:

Now you are going to alternate between the fpdc stitch and a dc stitch across the row. Keep track and make sure you are alternating or the pattern will not look right and you will have to start over. Once the row is complete, ch 3, then dc in the next stitch, and fpdc in the next stitch. Again you are going to alternate between dc and fpdc, the dc will end up in each fpdc from the last row, and the fpdc will end up in the dc from the previous row. Continue alternating until the row is complete.

Now ch 3, and repeat the pattern of dc and fpdc, making sure each dc is completed in an fpdc, and each fpdc is completed in a dc. Continue until the end of the row.

Continue repeating this row alternation and pattern until you have created a square similar in size to the others you have. Now you know how to do the waffle stitch! Crochet a few of these for your sampler then move on to the next awesome stitch!

Here is a picture of a completed square done in the waffle stitch:

The waffle knit is textured and a bit bulky but using a lighter weight yarn such as sport yarn will make it softer and lighter for making scarves and shawls. This stitch is close-knit and the tight stitches keep cold air from blowing through, it works great for blankets and lap blankets.

The texture is perfect for pillows too. Try making 2 of your squares at least 20-inch square. Sew them inside out together with a large plastic yarn needle. Stuff it with some poly-fluff filling and you will have yourself a nice pillow.

You can even make covers for the pillow you already have, don't stuff it, fold in the side you are going to leave open. When you are finished, insert your pillow and pull the folded piece over the end to hide the opening!

The Bullion Stitch

The bullion stitch is a thick textured stitch that is perfect for blankets and scarves. To create the bullion stitch with ease, make sure you yo or wrap your yarn loosely around the hook. This makes it easier to pull the hook and yarn through the loops without getting caught up.

This stitch can be worked straight up and down in rows, or it can be worked across by skipping a few stitches between the beginning and end of the bullion stitch. This is also used in embroidery and it can be used the same way on a finished crochet project to add interest by using yarn to embroider a design.

The stitch you are learning now is worked in every stitch across. This will give you bullion that is straight up and down across the row. Remember to work loose but not too loose, you want to be able to pull the yarn through your wraps without getting it stuck or unraveling it.

Step 1

This stitch is created by wrapping the yarn around, or multiple yo's. Ch 20 then ch 1 and turn, now yo 5 times or the number of times in your pattern.

Step 2

Put your hook into the next ch st and then yo and pull through all the loops on the hook.

Step 3

Yo and sc 1 then yo 5 and put your hook into the next ch st and then yo and pull through all the loops on the hook, go slowly to avoid getting stuck.

Step 4

Continue creating bullion stitches until you reach the end of the row then ch 1 and repeat steps 1–3 until you reach the desired length.

Here are a few finished rows of crochet using the bullion stitch.

Chapter 11: Advanced Crochet Patterns

Pineapple Lace

This is different from the fruit which it is named after and it's made up of the simplest stitches though it looks so fancy.

Bullion Stitch

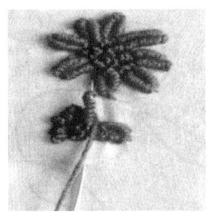

Go with the bullion stitch if you want a stitch whose texture is heavy. Pulling the hook through them all at one and working which quite a big amount of yarn overs, you will get lots of yarn bursts which are almost like 3D.

Loop Stitch

We expect the loop stitch to get its shining moment since tassels are having a moment, it's a fur on adorable amigurumi projects and great at embellishing accessories and pillows.

Crocodile Stitch

This crocodile stitch knows how to make a splash though it's so new to the world of crochet. And to give more stability to everything, you work the scales over a background of mesh. It can be useful in making jewelry, edgings, and pillows.

Starting and Finishing Project

Starting Project

Before making any stitches, it's important to understand how to hold a crochet hook. Part of this is determined by handedness; left-handed individuals don't have to learn to crochet in a typical manner (i.e. holding the hook in the right hand,) but they should keep in mind that most patterns are written for right-handed crochets.

This may make it worthwhile to learn to crochet with the right hand, but directions can be reversed with practice, so left-handers are under no duress to use their non-dominant hand. Because the majority of individuals are right-handed, this work focuses on learning to crochet with the right hand.

Ways to hold a crochet hook are numerous, but the 2 most common are referred to as the knife hold and the pencil hold. Neither is better than the other, only different. New crochets are encouraged to try both holds to find the one that is the most comfortable for them.

With the knife hold, the hand faces downward with the hook under the palm, much the way one would hold a knife. The pencil hold is the opposite: The palm faces upward with the hook grasped between the thumb and 2 forefingers, like holding a pencil.

Finishing Project

Properly finishing a crocheted piece is important for several reasons. First, the finishing process will settle the stitches, giving the piece a professional look. Second, finishing allows the crocheted to form the piece into the correct shape and straighten any shaping issues. Third, finishing items properly makes seaming and adding embellishments easier. Any way you look at it, then, finishing is a necessary part of the crocheting process.

The 2 main steps in finishing are weaving in the yarn ends and blocking. While many crafters don't see either process as particularly "fun," learning to perform them properly does take some of the anxiety out of the work. Hopefully, after finishing a few projects, blocking and weaving in ends will start to feel like just one more step in a crochet project.

Weaving in Ends

Every piece will have a yarn tail at the beginning and end of the work. Those crochet projects that have multiple yarn joins or colors will have more. For projects with many yarn tails, yarn ends should be woven in during the crocheting if at all possible, simply because leaving them all to the end can make the weaving process seem like a herculean task. The crocheted should also always leave at least a 6-inch tail of yarn; any shorter, and it may be too difficult to 'hide' the yarn inside the work.

In crocheting, there are 2 popular methods of weaving in ends: crocheting over them and weaving them in with a yarn needle. Both ways give desirable results, so it's up to crochets to decide which method they prefer.

New crochets should remember, however, that if their favorite method isn't working for a project, it's okay to try the other way.

Crocheting over yarn ends is performed exactly as it sounds: The crocheted places the yarn tail along the row of crochet stitches being worked and crochets over it with the stitches. Many crochets prefer this method simply because it doesn't leave the yarn tails to the end of the project. Of course, crocheting over yarn ends can also be tricky—circular motifs with many open areas, for example, might not lend themselves to this method. In these cases, it's also possible to crochet the yarn tail into the piece; the tail is held along with the working yarn, and the crocheted works as normal until the tail is used up.

Above: Crocheting Over Yarn Ends

Weaving in ends with a yarn needle can take longer, but it is a useful method to know for hiding ends in "tricky" areas. The goal is to secure the end as much as possible while ensuring that it can't be seen. The end should always be woven into the wrong side of the work; for works that have no "wrong" side (such as scarves,) the crocheted will have to choose a side.

To weave in the end with a yarn needle, the crocheted can run the yarn under a line of stitches for about an inch or so. Then, instead of snipping the yarn, the crocheted runs the tailback under half of the stitches. Before snipping the yarn, it's also helpful to pull the end taut so that it springs into position under the stitches.

Chapter 12: Basic Stitch Guide

Crochet is a simple art to acquire, as you only need to learn certain stitches to create a wide range of different creations. You can figure out how to make a crochet chain and slip stitch in a quick time to begin your projects, and then you have to learn at least one fundamental stitch. Then you will eventually have a sweater, a scarf, a shawl, or a sleeping bag!

Slip Stitch

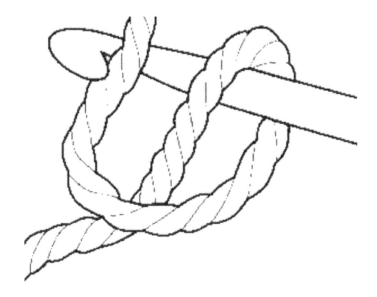

- Using your yarn, make a loop and insert the hook into the loop.

- Hook another loop through the first one.

- Tighten the slip knot and slip it up to your hook and you have a slip knot or slip stitch.

Half Double Crochet

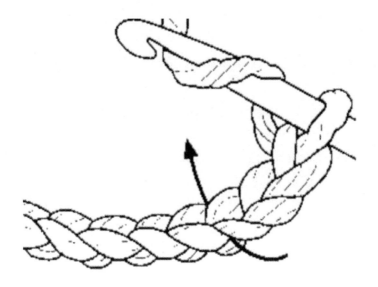

- YO your hook and into the 3rd chain from the hook.

- Yarn over and into the 3rd chain and you will have 3 loops.

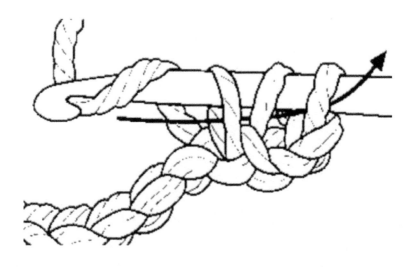

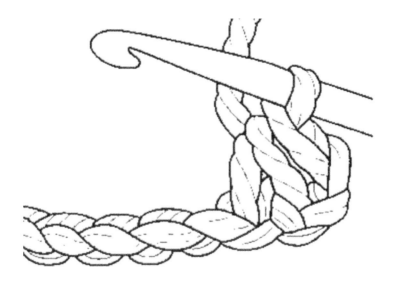

- YO and into the 3 loops; that is a half double crochet stitch.

- YO, insert your hook into the following chain and repeat from step 2.

Treble Crochet Stitch

1. YO twice and insert the hook into the 5th stitch.

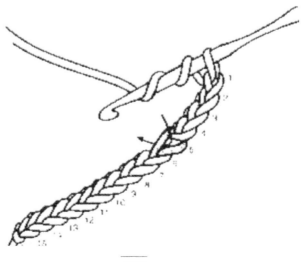

2. YO and draw it into the chain stitch and you will have 4 loops.

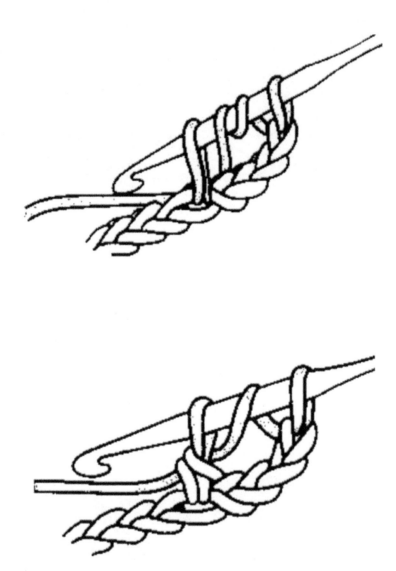

3. YO, draw through the first 2 loops and you will have 3 loops.

4. YO and into the first 2 loops on your hook and you will now have 2 loops.

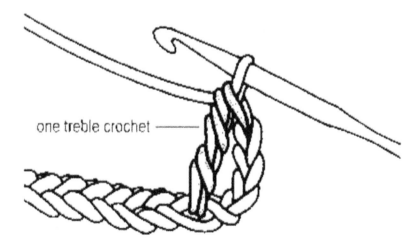

one treble crochet

5. YO and into the remaining 2 loops and you have treble crochet.

Single Crochet Stitch

Single crochet is the shortest and most basic of all stitches.

How to Single Crochet Row 1

1. Create chain 6 and slip the knot. Skip the first chain out of the crochet loop, push the loop into the secondary chain via the middle of the V and underneath the chain's back bar. Bring the thread from rear to front across the hook.

2. Draw yarn via the chain further up to the crochet hook's working place. Then you have 2 hook loops.

3. Again, bring the yarn over the hook from back to front, and draw it through both loops on the crochet hook.

4. One loop will remain on the hook; you have made one single crochet.

5. Place hook as before into the next thread, loop the yarn from back to front and draw it across the stitch of the thread. Yarn over again and bring both loops to open. Understanding that the words "hook" and "yarn over" have the same meaning, is significant. In both cases, you will carry the yarn from back to front over the hook. In each residual chain, repeat step 3, taking care to operate over the last chain though not in the slip knot. Remember to be vigilant not to bend the chain when you're working; keep all the Vs up against you. You've accomplished one single crochet thread, and now you will have 5 stitches in the thread.

How to Single Crochet Row 2

1. You have to flip the job counterclockwise to create the 2nd row of single crochet, as shown in the figure below, therefore you can work back through the first row.

2. Do not detach the crochet needle from the loop as this is shown in the figure below. Now just to execute the first stitch you must hold the yarn up to the appropriate height. Thus, chain 1 (it is considered a turning chain) to raise the thread.

3. That row along with all the preceding single crochet rows will be incorporated into some kind of former single crochet row, not the starting chain like you did previously. Keep in mind that you threaded the crochet hook through the middle of the V and below the bar while you were working through the initiating row. This is achieved only when you work through a starting sequence.

4. The very first single crochet throughout the row is employed over the last stitch of the preceding row (see figure below), not within the start chain.

5. Insert hook beneath the top 2 loops over the last stitch of the preceding row, carry the yarn over the hook from back to front, and pull yarn via stitch and up to the crochet hook work area. You've got 2 hook loops on already. Pull the yarn back to front over the hook afterward, and draw it onto the crochet hook around both loops.

6. Do single crochet for each crochet to that of the end, trying to take care of working in-stitch, particularly the last stitch, which can be easily missed (refer to the figure below).

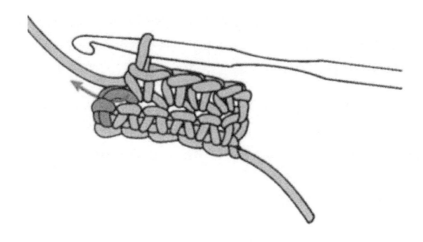

Let's take a pause now and counting the stitches; there are already 5 single crochets on the thread.

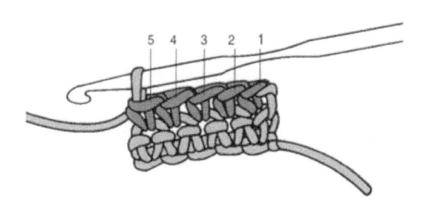

Fastening Off

Break the yarn after the last stitch, preserving a 6" top. Like you do when you take your crochet hook out for a rest, pull the hook straight ahead, but pull the cut yarn end via the stitch entirely this time. Tightly pull to close the 6-inch edge.

V Stitch

The V stitch is a very versatile stitch used in a lot of projects. To crochet a V stitch work a double crochet stitch in the next stitch, chain one, and then work another double crochet into the SAME stitch. Skip the next stitch and repeat.

Picot Stitch

Some patterns use "p" to symbolize a picot stitch. Picots are used to add decoration to a pattern and sometimes as fillers.

1. On the area where you're planning to add a picot stitch, do 3 chain stitches. Insert your hook into the 3rd chain from your loop. Sl st to close the stitch.

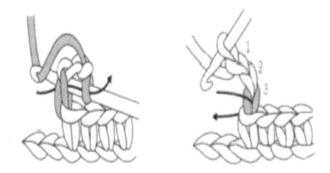

2. Add the picot stitches to the areas where you need to put them.

Double Crochet Stitch

The double crochet stitch is among the crochet stitches most widely utilized and is regarded as one of the simple stitches that are important. It's an incredibly useful stitch used in most designs on crochet. It creates a sturdy fabric, but not as rigid as a crocheted one using the single crochet stitch. Once you have grasped it, you can in no time make afghans, shawls, sweaters, and much more. The double crochet is approximately double the size of the single crochet stitch and is very simple to understand. It is shortened (dc) in crochet designs and has the T as a symbol in charts or diagrams, with a diagonal dash in the center.

1. Begin With Your Foundation Chain

You need something to incorporate with your double crochet stitches (except if you pick a dual crochet chainless base). So you have to start by crocheting a chain of foundation. Begin with a slip knot. Furthermore, just crochet the chain. When you deal with such a crochet design, the pattern will give you information regarding the length of your foundation chain. If you don't have a pattern to work with, you'll crochet a chain that is as long as you like for your project, potentially adding 2 more stitches. Let's just assume you would like to crochet a thin scarf, for example, which is 10 double crochet stitches throughout.

The possible explanation you're adding extra chains is that they're going to count as the very first double crochet that you might see in a moment.

2. Yarn Over and Insert Hook into Chain

Yarn over the hook, after which introduce the hook into the chain. On that first stitch, you're going to incorporate the hook into the 3rd chain from your hook.

Those chains you're going to skip are what you're using for your first double crochet row, even though you certainly won't be able to see it again until you've finished the next stitch. That's why you're adding those extra chains to the base chain as explained above, however, since they help to make the chains that will become the first double crochet. In the meantime, though, you can only believe that's the method you do it, so yarn it over and push the loop from the hook into the 3rd chain.

3. Yarn Over Again and Pull Through

Yarn over again, and then remove the yarn from those in the hook where you put your hook into the 3rd chain. You ought to see 3 loops in your crochet hook after you've accomplished the stage.

4. Yarn Over and Pull-Through 2 Loops on Hook

Yarn over again. Draw your yarn through the first 2 of the 3 loops on your hook. At the end of this stage, it will leave 2 loops on the hook.

5. Yarn Over and Complete the Stitch

Yarn for the last time. Draw both loops which are both on the line. You've done stitching double crochet. When you've accomplished the first double crochet stitch, you can see it stands to the right of what seems to be some other double crochet stitch; this is the stitch that was made while you omitted the first 3 chains as they behave as the first double crochet stitch during the first row.

6. Completing the Row of Double Crochet Stitches

Only at the very start of the base row you just need to miss the first 3 strings. You needn't skip chains after that. So, with your next double crochet, you're going to follow the same steps described above, except you're going to insert the hook into the next stitch which is immediately left of the original double crochet thread. You will continue to do so by inserting a double crochet stitch to each chain before the end of the string.

7. Turning Chain of 3

As described in step 6, other than at the very starting of the base chain, you don't have to miss any links, to create the project's first double crochet. Indeed, you will have to build a turning chain every time you turn the work and start a new path. It's similar in that you're doing all the row's first double crochet without any of the steps of a double crochet stitch literally. You'll be chaining 3 to do this. That is going to count as your first dc in that sequence. So you're going to figure out the next double crochet by turning the yarn over and putting the stitch into the next one.

8. Working Into Front and Back Loops Only (Optional)

The measures above explain how double crochet stitch rows can be crocheted. Several items can be changed to make distinctly different patterns using the double crochet stitch though. The most common of these is that you can either crochet the stitch in the front loops, or just each row's back loops. Still using the fundamental dc stitch, it will produce different textures, tension, and ribbing choices.

Chapter 13: Blocking Your Crochet

Blocking is a vital part of the crochet process as it is the part that makes your projects look professional. It is sometimes termed as "dressing" the project and we use moisture and, on occasion, heat to finish it. If you are making garments, correct blocking can go an awful and long way towards making the garment fit properly and making it look better. It can also help Afghans or rugs that have become misshapen regain their symmetry.

Blocking sets the stitches in place and enhance the way the fabric drapes. It is much easier to seam and edge on a blocked piece and, if needed, you can also make any minor adjustments to size while you are blocking as well.

There are a few different methods to blocking crochet and you need to know which one works for the project you need to block, otherwise, your result will not be what you expect and you could find that all your hard work has gone to waste.

The method you use depends on the item itself and the yarn or thread that has been used to crochet it. Some items cannot be blocked, like 3D pieces that are not easy to handle, or very small items. Some fibers are not ideal for blocking either.

Getting Started

First of all, you need to get some supplies ready. Do this before you start crocheting your project so that, when you have gathered your supplies, you are all set to go? You will need:

- A blocking board—must be flat and large enough to hold what you want to block. Pieces should not be allowed to hang off the edge of the blocking board.

- Rustproof pins—important—if you don't get the rustproof ones you might find rust marks on your work when you have finished blocking.

- Steamer or steam iron.

- Spray bottle.

- The labels from your yarn or thread.

If you can't find or your budget doesn't allow a commercial blocking board, you can easily make one. All you need is a large piece of plastic foam insulation board, which you can get from an office supply or DIY store. When you are choosing which size to buy, keep in mind that while a huge board can be used to block several pieces, it is more difficult to store. Perhaps consider buying several boards of different sizes.

Cover the board over with a thick towel and then a cotton cloth or cotton sheet. Do wash both of these first to ensure that they do not "bleed" onto your work. Solid white is often the best color to go for but you can use a fabric that has stripes or a large check print so that you can use the lines as a guide for your blocking.

Place your board in a room where it can be left undisturbed while you are blocking. This might be just a few minutes or it can be an entire day or 2, depending on the size of the piece and the yarn used. The board must be able to take pins, heat, and moisture. If you have large items, like large Afghans or blankets, you could use a bed or a padded dining room table. If not, you can always cover part of a carpeted floor in a sheet and use that.

Blocking Methods

You may hear of blocking methods being described as wet, cold, or dry. The method you choose will depend on the content of the yarn, the final use, and your preferred method.

The first step is to look at the label that came with the yarn to see what fibers have been used. Sometimes a skein will contain many different fibers and, if that is the case, the most delicate of the fibers must take precedence. Most of the natural fibers, like wool, cotton, mohair, or linen, can be wet or dry blocked. Some of the synthetic fibers do not gain any benefit from being blocked and can be ruined if you are not careful. If you have used metallic or novelty fibers, these need special attention and might not be able to be blocked at all.

If possible, make up a test swatch of the yarn you are using to check for the gauge and to practice blocking on. This will ensure that you are using the right method for it. If you are using acrylic yarn, it might interest you to know that too much heat can actually "kill it," making it go limp and shiny. It's better to ruin your swatch than your project!

Wet Blocking

Wet blocking can only be used on fibers that can be submerged in water. Wash your swatch and see what happens to it. If the material does not hold up to washing, it cannot be wet blocked. If you are ready to start wet blocking, wash the piece first or wet it thoroughly and squeeze the excess water out gently. Do not twist or wring the material. If the piece is 2D, lay it out flat on the blocking board, and pat it into shape gently. Make sure you shape it to the dimensions you want it to be when finished because once the blocking is over, it can't be undone.

When you are satisfied, pin the piece securely to the board. If it is a 3D piece, stuff it with rolled-up plastic bags or another stuffing that is waterproof. If the piece is round, blow a balloon up inside the piece to the desired size. Leave it alone to dry completely. You can speed this up by having a fan blowing over the piece but not set up right on top of it.

Dry Blocking

Dry blocking can be used on those fibers that can take both moisture and heat in the form of steam. Pin the piece onto the board in your desired shape or measurements. Keep the pins close together and spaced out evenly so the fabric does not get distorted.

Smooth out all of the seams and any areas that have become puckered or rippled—do this with your fingers. Hold a steam iron or steamer above the piece about an inch or so away, and steam the fabric completely and thoroughly—DO NOT LET THE IRON TOUCH THE FABRIC. Leave the piece alone to cool off and dry.

Cold Blocking

Cold blocking is ideal for those fibers that can tolerate moisture but can't tolerate heat. Pin the piece to the board in the same way as you did for dry blocking. Fill a spray bottle with clean water and mist it over the piece until it is completely wet. Use extra pins if there are areas that refuse to lie flat or press them down with your (clean) hands for a minute. Leave it until it is dry.

Blocking Tips for Large Pieces

• Large pieces, such as Afghans, blankets, tablecloths, or shawls, can be blocked on a bed that has a good firm or extra-firm mattress. You can also pad your dining table with a blanket and cover it or use a covered clean floor with carpet.

• Arrange your piece so it is a nice and even shape. Do not overstretch it and do not distort the shape. Pin it down securely, keeping the pins evenly spaced but close together. Add some extra pins to stubborn bits that just won't lie flat.

• Dry block or block with no heat. Use the instructions above for dry blocking or you can mist it thoroughly with chemical-free water until it is semi-saturated (not sopping wet). Use your hand to press each area as you spray it and let the heat from your skin act as iron at low temperature. This is a great way of blocking without the damage that can be caused by iron.

• Once you have wet and hand-pressed it, set up a fan to blow over it gently until it is dry.

Now that you know how to block your work, you will have the confidence to take that final step; the step that will make your work look finished and professional.

Chapter 14: Easy Crochet Projects

Barefoot Sandals

They're so cute! Imagine you are going to the beach or swimming pool and you are wearing your own handmade and barefoot sandals. You can pin these colors to match your mood and attire. First, you can make an ankle strap, and then create a triangular shape of sandals sewn to the center of the first chain of 3 spaces by sliding.

This will naturally reduce the line until you form a point in your thumb. Before crochet, the initial loop glides the button on the yarn, and when the crochet is made. When knitting a button opening, it puts it in the right position.

The gauge is not important for this project.

Materials you will need:

- 1 ball of lion brand micro-spinning in lavender.

- Size G/6 (4 mm.) crochet.

- Tapestry needles, woven at the end.

Note: If the piece is too long, the leg skips line 8 through the working slip to the center of the 2nd place on the row, then runs on line 9.

Chain 6 is associated with a slip seam, forming a button aperture loop.

- **Line 1:** Chain 36, sliding button-down and away at the end of the line, single crochet in the 2nd chain from the hook and cross to the ring for the strap on the ankle, end of crochet in the 2nd chain from the hook, and across to the ankle strap ring, end-35 pins.

- **Line 2:** The last pin on the front loop, the 11th pin, one crochet connects the yarn with one crochet, the next loop 14 PIN-15 pins.

- **Line 3:** Chain 6 (counting dc and chain 3 space), skip 1 pin, dc in the next stitch, chain 3, span-8 dc, and 7 circuit space.

- **Line 4:** Slip to the center of the first chain 3 space, chain 6 (counting dc and chain 3 space), dc in the center of the chain 3 space, (Chain 3, dc in the lower circuit 3 space) through, leaving the remaining stitches do not work, 7 dc and 6 chain Space.

- **Line 5:** Repeat lines 4–6 dc and 5 chain space.

- **Line 6:** Repeat lines 4–5 dc and 4 chain space.

- **Line 7:** Repeat lines 4–4 dc and 3 chain space.

- **Line 8:** Slip to the center of the first Circuit 3 space, chain 3 (Countdown dc), dc in the center under the chain 3 space twice-3 dc.

- **Line 9:** First PIN-slip, central dc single crochet.

- **Line 10:** Twist, one crochet in one crochet.

- **Line 11:** Bend, single crochet in one crochet, chain 8, slip pin in the same crochet for toe ring, end.

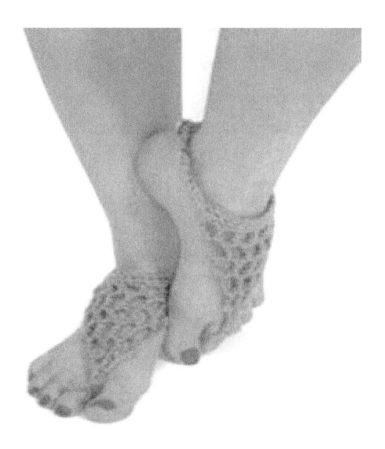

Hand Towels

Crochet towels are handy in the kitchen, and they can be used for a variety of purposes, like keeping them near the washing sink. Moreover, hand towels make a great. So let's get started with the easy crochet instructions to make your kitchen hand towel.

Finish size: 10.5x18-inches (26.5-x46 cm.)

Materials you will need:

- Ball(s) of knit pick cotlin yarn, depending on the colors you want to prefer. Use more colors to make a striped hand towel.

- H crochet hook of 5.5 mm. size.

- Tapestry needle.

- Scissor.

- Sewing needle and thread (optional).

- Button (optional).

- Yarn needle.

Gauge: 14 rows and 12 stitches as 4 inches (10 cm.) in the pattern.

How to do

• To make this crochet hand towel, you should know how to do pique stitch. It is quite simple to work with—just yarn over (yo) and then insert hook into the 3rd chain (ch-3) from the hook; you can also do this from the first stitch (st) of the row.

• Yarn over (yo) and then draw a loop. Make 3 loops on the hook, and your stitch will look like a double crochet stitch (dc). Then yarn over (yo) and draw it through the 3 loops; in this way, you will have 2 loops on the hook.

• Yarn over (yo) to insert the hook into the same chain, and draw up a loop; in this way, you will have 4 loops. It will your first complete pique stitch.

• Now, you these instructions for pique stitch to crochet a hand towel.

• If you are thinking of making a striped hand towel, here's how you can lose a chain for a starting chain.

• **Row 1:** Starting from the 3rd chain (ch-3), work a pique stitch in every 30 stitches (sts).

• **Row 2:** Single crochet stitch (sc) in every stitch (st). Then work in chain 2 (ch-2) for a turning chain and turn.

• **Row 3:** Now pique stitch in every stitch and then work chain 1 (ch-1) for a turning chain and turn.

• Repeat row 2, row 3, and row 4 and then change to the new yarn, e.g., color 1.

• Then repeat row 3 and row 2, 2 times and change to another color yarn, e.g., color 2.

• Now, repeat row 3 and row 2, 1 time and then change to a different color yarn, e.g., color 3.

• Repeat row 3 and row 2, 2 times, change to the color 2 yarn, and then repeat row 3 and row 2 one time.

• Change to a different color yarn, e.g., color 4, and repeat row 3 and row 2, 2 times.

• Change to the color 2 yarn and then repeat row 3 and row 2, 7 times.

• Change to the floor 4 yarn and then and then repeat row 3 and row 2, 2 times.

• Change to the color 2 yarn and then repeat row 3 and row 2, 1 time.

• Change to the color 3 yarn and then repeat row 3 and row 2, 2 times.

• Change to the color 2 yarn and then repeat row 3 and row 2, 1 time.

• Change to the color 1 yarn and then repeat row 3 and row 2, 2 times.

• Change to the color 2 yarn and then repeat row 3 and row 2, 3 times.

• Now, you are done; secure the last stitch, trim the yarn and weave in all the ends.

• You can also crochet a hanging loop to attach it around the kitchen like on a cabinet handle or hook. For this, make a tail and to make it, when you reach the upper left corner of the towel, slip stitch (sl st) in the chain 5 (ch-5) from the hook to make a button loop. Then slip stitch (sl st) in the remaining chains and work back towards the kitchen towel. When done, slip stitch (sl st) in the single crochet stitch (sc) at the corner and secure the last stitch, and trim it. Now, weave this tail through the 2 rows of the hand towel and then sew the button. Secure the yarn and weave in loose ends by using a yarn needle.

Coffee Sleeve

Do you love coffee to death?

Indeed, there is nothing pleasurable than enjoy a mug of hot coffee at a crisp temperature. Even in the morning don't seem energetic until you had coffee. What if your coffee can get its little cozy sweater? Here's how you can quickly crochet a cute and easy coffee sleeve, which will take only 10 minutes.

And, this crochet coffee sweeter is also a perfect last minute that you can whip up for someone who is always glued to the Starbucks cup. Although this coffee sleeve isn't actually for just a Starbucks cup, it goes great with all types of coffee mugs like travel mugs, water bottles, beer/soda can, even with cold beverages. And, once you come to know to crochet one, you can customize the pattern as you want.

Let's begin with a simple pattern—a crooked coffee sleeve that is perfect for crochet enthusiastic at a beginner level. In this way, you will get to take your crochet skills to another level.

Finish size: Standard coffee mug (16 oz.)

Materials you will need:

- Ball of worsted weight yarn (any color).

- H crochet hook of 5.0 mm. size.

- Scissor.

- Yarn needle.

How to do:

- **Row 1:** Yarn over (yo) and then draw a loop. Work in 2 single crochet stitches (sc) in the 2nd (ch-2) from hook, make one single crochet stitch (sc) across the last 2 stitches, single crochet 2 together (sc2tog), then chain 1 (ch-1), and turn.

- **Row 2:** Single crochet 2 together (sc2tog) and single crochet stitch (sc) across the last stitch, then make 2 single crochets in the last stitch, channel 1(ch-1), and turn.

- **Row 3:** Work in 2 single crochet stitch (sc) in first single crochet stitch (sc), then single crochet stitch (sc) across last 2 stitches, single crochet 2 together (sc2tog), then chain 1 and turn.

- **Row 4:** Repeat instructions in row 2 and 3.

- **Row 5:** Repeat instructions in row 2 and 3.

- **Row 6:** Repeat instructions in row 2 and 3.

- ...

- ...

- ...

- ...

- **Row 24:** Repeat instructions in row 2 and 3.

- In this way, you will get an 8-inch long piece. Join the ends of the piece with a whip stitch or slip stitch (sl st) and then slip it right-side-out.

Basket Weave Coffee Sleeve

Materials you will need:

- 1 (50 g.) ball of yarn (any color).

- N crochet hook (4.5 mm.).

- Scissor.

- Yarn needle.

- Sewing needle and thread (optional).

- Button (optional)

How to do:

- You must know the front post double crochet stitch (FPdc) and back post double crochet stitch (BPdc). To do it, yarn over (yo) and then draw a loop by inserting hook from front to back and then to front around specified double crochet. Then yarn over (yo), draw through 2 loops, repeat this step twice, and front post double crochet is made.

- For back post double crochet stitch (BPdc), yarn over (yo), and then draw a loop by inserting hook from back to front and then to back around specified double crochet. Then yarn over (yo), draw through 2 loops, repeat this step twice, and back post double crochet is made.

- **Row 1:** Work in chain 30 (ch-30), join with a slip stitch (sl st) and form a ring.

- **Row 2:** Work in chain 3 (ch-3); it will count as double crochet stitch (dc), work in one double crochet in each stitch (st) around, and then join with a slip stitch (sl st) on top of the chain 3 (ch-3).

- **Row 3:** Work in chain 3 (ch-3), work in front post double crochet stitch (FPdc) in the next 2 stitches (sts), *back post double crochet stitch (BPdc) in the next 3 stitches (sts), front post double crochet stitch (FPdc) in the next 3 stitches (sts)*, repeat * to * for 4 times, back post double crochet stitch (BPdc) in the next 3 stitches and then join with a slip stitch (sl st) on top of chain 3 (ch-3).

- **Row 4:** Repeat row 3.

- **Row 5:** Work in chain 3 (ch-3), work in back post double crochet stitch (BPdc) in the next 2 stitches (sts), * front post double crochet stitch (FPdc) in the next 3 stitches (sts), *back post double crochet stitch (BPdc) in the next 3 stitches (sts)*, repeat * to * for 4 times, front post double crochet stitch (FPdc) in the last 3 stitches (sts) and then join with a slip stitch (sl st) on top of chain 3 (ch-3).

- **Row 6:** Repeat row 5.

- **Row 7:** Repeat row 5.

- **Row 8:** Repeat row 3.

- **Row 9:** Repeat row 3.

- **Row 10:** Repeat row 3.

- When done, secure the last stitch, trim it, then secure the yarn and weave in loose ends by using a yarn needle. In the end, sew a button into the sleeve if desired.

Coffee Sleeve with Wooden Button

Another easy pattern for a coffee sleeve is dressed with a button stylishly.

Materials you will need:

- Ball of chunky yarn (any color).

- N crochet hook of 5.5 mm size.

- Scissors.

- Wooden button.

- Yarn needle.

- Embroidery floss.

- Sewing needle and thread (optional)

How to do:

- **Row 1:** Yarn over (yo) and then draw a loop. Work in chain 2 (ch-2), and then half double crochet stitch (hdc) in each chain until the end of round; don't join the end. Then, place a stitch marker in the last stitch and continue working continuously in a spiral.

- **Row 2:** Half double crochet stitch (hdc) in each chain until the end of the round and then replace the stitch marker in the last stitch.

- **Row 3:** Half double crochet stitch (hdc) in each chain until the end of the round and then replace the stitch marker in the last stitch.

- **Row 4:** Half double crochet stitch (hdc) in each chain until the end of the round and then replace the stitch marker in the last stitch.

- ...

- ...

- ...

- **Row 8:** Half double crochet stitch (hdc) in each chain until the end of the round and then replace the stitch marker in the last stitch.

- When done, secure the last stitch, trim it, then secure the yarn and weave in loose ends by using a yarn needle. In the end, attach a wooden button by using embroidery floss or just sew it into the sleeve.

Easy Peasy Pompom Hat

I just had to turn on this cute model. This perfect hat for any girl or boy, modeling shows a little boy wearing a blue hat, but you can easily change the color for a little girl. The pattern is written in small scale (to fit the head of the child 3/6 (6/12–18/24) and the bond is of great size. The hat is served as a single piece and then folds the pieces and stitched to the side and top of the semes to form the hat. Attach a pukhraj to each corner and have a nice look for every child in your life.

Gauge: 12 single crochets and 13 rows of equal 4-inch.

Materials you will need:

- 1 ball from the caron just to sew a baby obra yarn to the end of a sailor boy's vested.

- A size g/10 (6 mm) crochet hook.

- A silk needle at the end.

How to do:

- Pat's last line to work with the prayer system 6 (7–8) inches. Your seat belt is chained.

- Cut into half and fold. Stitch a side and top.

- Pompom (Make 2).

- Wrap around 50 times the thread of 3 fingers. Remove the finger and tie it tightly in the center. Cut the loop on each side. Smooth circle shape. 1 pompom stitched in every corner of the hat.

Chapter 15: Baby Crochet Projects

To put what you have learned into practice, here are some easy and amazing baby crochet projects that you could try!

Baby's First Crochet Hat

Perfect for newborns, this is so warm and comforting!

Yarn weight: 3 (Light/DK).

Crochet hook: 6mm/J.

Instructions:

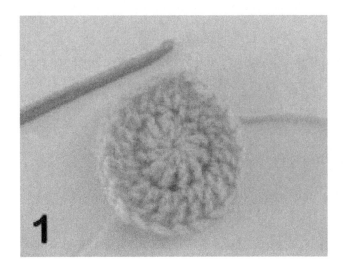

- **Round 1:** Create a circle then make ch 3 and 11 dc in the said circle until 12 stitches.

- **Round 2:** Make 1 dc and ch 3 in the first stitch then 2 dc in every stitch all the way around until you reach 24 stitches.

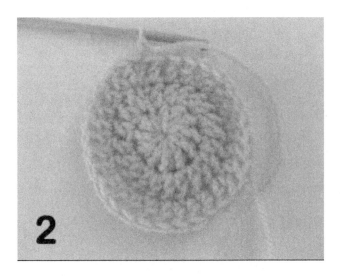

- **Round 3:** Next, make ch 3 and 2 dc in the next stitch. *Make 1 dc in the next stitch and 2 dc in the other* then repeat from * to * all the way around until it reaches 3 1/2-inches.

- **Round 4–10**: Ch 3 in 1 dc for every stitch in the round.

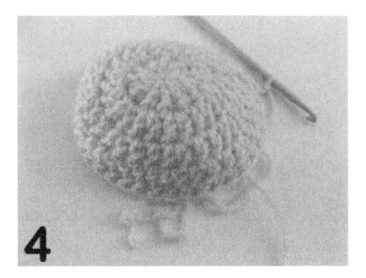

- **Round 11:** Make ch 1 and 1 sc for each stitch. *Then, make 1 sc for each of the next 8 stitches and 2 sc in the next* Repeat from * to * all the way and make sl stitch to join.

- **Round 12 onwards:** Make 1 sc and ch 1 for every stitch in the round and then continue until you reach the diameter that would suit the baby's head.

Baby Booties

Soft, wrap-around booties that are sure to make babies feel good and ready to go!

Yarn Weight: 4 (Medium eight/Aran).

Crochet Hook: 4 mm. or 6/G.

Instructions:

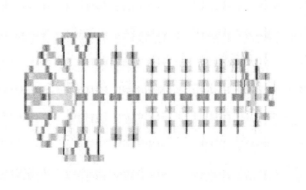

Sole

- Make 11 ch.

- **Round 1:** Make sc in 2nd chain, then single chain 5 times, make 3 hdc, and 7 hdc in the last chain. Work the rest of the round from the back of the chain before making hdc thrice, then single chain 5 times, and 4 in the last chain. Slip stitch to first st to make 28 stitches.

- **Round 2:** Sc in the same sc to make ch 1, then sc 7 times before making hdc, make 2 hdc thrice in a stitch, and then 2 hdc thrice again.

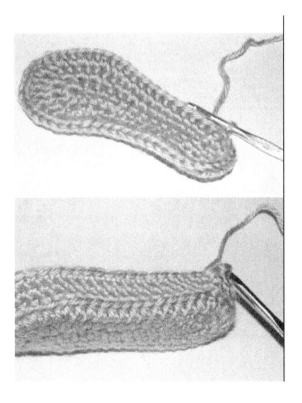

Shoe

- **Round 3:** Work in back loops while making ch 1, then sc in the same stitch and do so all the way round, sl st to join and make 39 stitches.

- **Round 4–5:** Make ch 1, sc in same sc, sc all the way around, double chain 2tog, dc3tog, double chain 2tog, sl stitch to single chain to make 33 stitches.

- **Round 7–8:** single chain in same sc 5 times, sc2tog, dc, dc3tog, single-chain 2 together before going all the way around, and weave ends in to make 23 stitches.

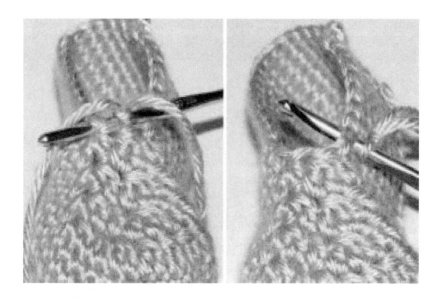

Boot Cuff

- **Round 1:** hdc 3rd chain from the hook, hdc 19 times and leave 3 spaces, and then work in opposite directions.

- **Round 2:** Make ch 2 and then turn, hdc for 28 times, ch 1 and then skip 1 hdc.

- **Round 3:** Ch 2, turn, make hdc, hdc in ch 1 space, hdc to make 32 stitches.

- **Round 4:** Make scallops by making 5 dc from the 2nd hdc *skip 1 sc, skip next hdc* Repeat * to * all the way around and then slip stitch to join.

Easy Baby Bib

Keep your baby's chin and clothes clean from food residue by making this easy, beautiful baby bib!

Yarn: Medium/approx. 50 yards.

Crochet hook: 5.50 mm.

Instructions:

- **Round 1:** Make chain 3, 8 hdc from the 3rd hook, and then make a slip stitch at the beginning of the 3rd chain

- **Round 2:** Make chain 2, and then turn, make 2 hdc in the next chain and continue all the way around, then sl st at the beginning of the 2nd round.

- **Round 3:** Make chain 2, and then turn, make 2 hdc in the next chain and continue all the way around, then sl st at the beginning of the 3rd round.

- **Round 4:** Ch 2, 2 hdc in the next sc, and then make another hdc, and sl stitch at the beginning of the next round.

- **Rounds 5–6:** Make ch 2 then turn around and sl st at the beginning of the next stitch.

- **Round 7:** Make ch 2 then turn before making 2 hdcs and then another hdc in the next 4 hdcs to make 49 hdc.

- **Round 8:** Make 4 ch, turn, make 2ch in the next hdc, then dc in the next hdc before making another 4 hdcs, make 2 ch in the next hdc, dc in the next 2 ch, and then make 2 hdcs to make 56 stitches.

Straps

- Make strap by making 25—or as many chains—as you want and then sl st to join.

Dainty Baby Sweater

Keep your child safe from the lingering cold with this dainty, easy to make a baby sweater that you're sure to love! You might even think of making some others give as gifts, too!

Yarn: 3-ply fingering/baby yarn.

Crochet Hook: 5.5 mm/GE.

Instructions:

Back

- **Round 1:** Make 49 ch, then dc in the 2nd loop from the hook, dc in each of the next 2 chains, and then turn to form 12 groups of 2 dcs.

- **Round 2:** Make ch 4, sc in the first ch space across, and then work to the last sc of the previous row, chain 3, and turn.

- **Round 3:** Make 2 dc in the first loop, make 1 ch, 3 dc in next ch, and then chain-loop across.

- **Round 4–23:** Repeat rounds 1–3, 10 times.

Front

- **Round 1:** Make ch 4, sc in the first ch-space, then chain 3, sc in the next chain thrice, chain 3 again, 4 chains, loop thrice.

- **Round 2:** Make a double chain in the first 3 chain loops. Make chain 1, 3 dc in the next loop thrice and then turn.

- **Rounds 3–23:** Repeat the first 2 rounds until they measure the same as the ones on the back and fasten off.

Collar and Facing:

- **Round 1:** Make 3 chains in the next space, and repeat the process around the entire fabric. Make sure to work on both front and back ends.

- **Round 2:** In the first space, make 3 dc, then make 4 dc in the next ch space, then join and turn.

- **Round 3:** Make 3 chains in the next space, and repeat the process around the entire fabric. Make sure to work on both front and back ends.

- **Round 4:** In the next space, make 3 dc, then make 4 dc in the next ch space, then join and turn.

- **Round 5:** Make another 3 chains in the next space, and repeat the process around the entire fabric. Make sure to work on both front and back ends.

- **Round 6:** Repeat rounds 2 and 4 but make 160 stitches.

- **Round 7–8:** Make chain 3 and then dc in the first ch space 48 times, ch 1 21 times3 dc in the next space, picot 27 times, dc 21 times, and then sl stitch to join.

Sleeves

- **Round 1:** Chain 4 and then sc in the next space, ch 3 13 times, ch 3 again, and turn.

- **Round 2:** Make 2 dc in the first chain, 3 dc-loop, and turn.

- **Rounds 3–15:** Repeat Rows 1 and 2.

- **Round 16:** Make 2 dc in the first 3-ch loop, picot, and then fasten off.

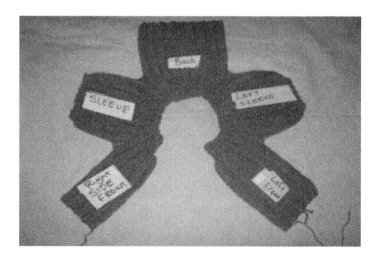

Finishing

- Sew the sleeves on and then fasten off the seams. Sew a ribbon in the middle.

Baby Cocoon

Babies are like butterflies, too! Let them stay in their cocoon to keep them safe from harsh weather conditions, and to take care of them better!

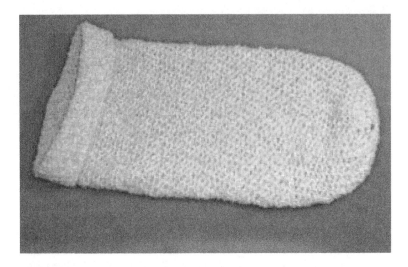

Yarn: 2 (Fine/23 to 26 inches).

Crochet Hook: 6mm or J/10.

Instructions:

- **Round 1:** Ch 3, then make 11 dc inside the ring, and join with sl st dc stitches.

- **Round 2:** Make 3 chains, 1 double crochet in the first dc, and then 2 dc in the next 2 dcs all the way around.

- **Round 3:** Make 3 chains, make 1 dc in each chain, and then make 2 dc *1 dc in the next 2 dcs, 2 dc in next dc*. Repeat * to * all the way to the end and join with slip stitches.

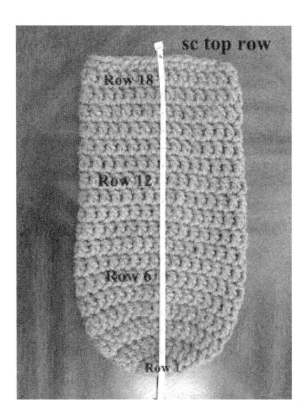

- **Round 4:** Make 3 chains, make 1 dc in each chain, and then make 2 dc *1 dc in the next 2 dcs, 2 dc in next dc*. Repeat * to * all the way to the end and join with slip stitches.

- **Round 5:** Make 1 ch, then single crochet in the same stitch and make 1 ch *Sc in the next dc in the first ch space* Repeat * to * all the way to the end.

- **Round 6:** Make 1 ch, and sc in the same stitch *Make ch 1 then skip single crochet in the next chain space* Repeat * to * until the end and finish off by burying or knotting ends.

Chapter 16: Tips and Tricks for Beginners

Crochet Tips and Tricks

1. To avoid balls of yarn from falling and rolling, place them in a reused hand wipe jar of cylindrical shape. Just like wipes, the yarn will also come out through the same hole.

2. Mark your rows by using a stitch marker, bobby pin, safety pin.

3. Store your crochet hooks in the jewelry box, pencil box, or traveling toothpaste holder. You can also hang your hooks on a small piece of wool. A multipurpose storage box is also a good option.

4. Highlight your pattern with different colors so that you can understand it easily. Underline different stitches. If your patterns demand rows of a different color, highlight the rows with the same color or with the colors that you have decided to use.

5. Always keep abbreviations, measurements, hook, and yarn weights table in printable forms so that you can easily use them whenever you want.

6. Use rapped or leftover yarns to make pompoms, Afghan squares, bracelets, and many more articles like these.

7. If you use homespun yarn for your pattern, then metal hooks are a better option than plastic ones.

8. If you love to do crochet during traveling, prepare a separate crochet box. Always have travel-friendly crochet tools, for example,

foldable scissors that are easy to carry and also will not snug the things in the bag.

9. Many crochet patterns do not go well with ironing. So instead of it, take an equal quantity of water and starch and spray the pattern with it and let it dry on a flat surface.

10. Store the crochet patterns in your notebook by using sheet protectors.

11. Make sure you sit in a proper position to provide enough support to your elbows, and hands during crocheting.

12. Take breaks after regular intervals to refresh yourself.

13. There is a variety of hand massage and stretching techniques. So do any of them that you find it easy to relax your hand muscles.

14. Using ergonomic crochet tools such as circular needles is also useful to avoid hand fatigue.

15. Use stress relief gloves.

16. Pick up your hook every day. The hardest part about learning how to crochet is training your hand to hold your hook (and the yarn) with the correct tension. Do not give up and keep in mind that practice makes perfect!

17. Begin with small projects. Learning how to crochet takes time and most of the time, beginners feel discouraged when they are not able to complete a project—I mean, who wouldn't? The best thing to do is to start with small attainable projects. There is no better feeling than completing your very first project. Start with small items such as

squares, mandalas, and coasters before moving onto larger projects such as blankets and cushions.

18. Chain, chain, chain. When learning to crochet, making several chains is the best way to improve your tension since they are the foundation of all stitches. You will be ready for stitches that are more complicated once all your chains look nice and even.

19. Make stitch swatches. You can work on small swatches to help you to familiarize yourself with the different stitches. You can even sew these swatches together to create face cloths or small blankets.

20. Avoid changing hooks in the middle of a project. Your stitches should be consistent throughout the whole project. When you switch hooks mid-project, you risk creating an inconsistency. Even changing the same size hooks from one manufacture to another can be problematic. This is because the size of the hook is not always the same between manufacturers and small changes in how the hooks are shaped can change the way you create your stitches or hold the hook hence the need for practice swatches.

Chapter 17: FAQ's

How to Hold the Hook When Crocheting

It is very important that the hook is held properly while doing crochet work. This will reduce the incidence of pain in your wrist and will even make your work go on smoothly. There are 2 major methods mentioned in crochet literature. They are the pencil hold and the knife hold.

- **The pencil hold:** One way of gripping your hook is by holding it with your thumb, index finger, and middle finger. You can just imitate the way you'll hold your writing pencil.

- **The knife hold:** You can also hold it like your knife, with your palm on the handle, your 3 fingers wrapped around it, and your index finger pointing towards the head of the hook.

Which of the 2 Methods Mentioned Above Is Better?

In the real sense, we all have different ways of handling stuff. We all hold our writing pencils differently, and it is part of what accounts for the differences in handwriting. 2 different people might also have different ways of holding the knife. So, I will say find the style that suits you and crochet away!

Right and Wrong Sides of a Crochet Piece

In the art of crochet, working on the wrong side might lead the crocheter into making errors and therefore result in frogging. Working on the wrong side can also give a crochet result that is entirely different from what the crocheter had in mind (or in the picture).

How do you avoid working on the wrong side of a crochet piece?

You can avoid this by not doing any crochet on the tail of the yarn. The tail of the yarn is the length of the yarn between your piece and the ball or skein of yarn. For the piece to be on the right side, the tail should be at the bottom right corner.

How to Differentiate the Front and Back of a Chain Stitch?

While some authorities will tell you to work from back to the front, others might instruct you to do the reverse. Also, while some will ask you to do the front loop only (flo), the back loop only (blo) might turn out to be the focus of some other instructional guides. Not following these instructions might lead to you ending up with a work that is different from what you had in mind before you started. The front of a loop looks like Vs sitting on top of one another while the back looks like humps.

Frogging (Undoing Crochet)

Frogging in crocheting terms simply means to correct an error. Stitches that have been crocheted in error can be ripped out and remade. You just have to be patient and gentle with the fabric when doing so. Frogging can both be easy and painful at the same time.

You just have to pull out your hook and rip it off till you get to the point where the error was made and just continue again. You can roll the frogged yarn into a ball or around the material to prevent it from tangling. What's most painful? You have no choice but to do it again as soon as frogging occurs! It is advisable to mark the point where you are to stop frogging with a stitch marker to avoid ripping beyond the necessary point.

When you are frogging, you should not be very fast with it. Instead, to make your frogging smooth, you need to be slow-paced enough to detach the stitches from the base of the stitch and not pulling upwards.

It is not impossible, that you have knots in your work (points where you had to join a piece of yarn to the other), and when you get to points like this, you should be careful to untie the knot first. If it is tightly tied and can't be untied, cut it off.

Crotchet can also be frogged entirely to reclaim it. You can decide to use the yarn to make something else, and so frogging becomes necessary.

Some Crocheting Mistakes and How to Avoid Them

Ruling out completely the possibility of errors in a beginner's work is impossible. Even people who have been doing crochet for a long time are still susceptible to some of these mistakes. These errors can, however, be mitigated. Some of these mistakes are:

- Using a different yarn weight from the one instructed: yarns are not all the same; they vary in color, materials, and weights. You should check the instructions to know the correct one to use so that you won't be 'wowed' by your crochet piece when it is done.

- Not counting your stitches and rows as you go along your crochet work. To lessen the pain (lol) that is often associated with frogging, try to count your rows and stitches as you work. A digital row counter can be of great help.

- Not understanding the how-to of a project before embarking on it. In relative terms, crochet work takes time. So, why not know what to do before you start? I will advise beginners to ALWAYS read through pattern instructions before putting the hook to the yarn.

This will help you to avoid unnecessary stress as you continue in the project. It will also help to reduce the incidence of frogging or even having to abandon the entire project.

- Working with one loop only: It is not uncommon for beginners to only slide the hooks under one of the loops and neglect the other one. Except the instruction says otherwise, it is better to work with both loops.

- Misplacing the first stitch. You should learn where to place the first stitches in each row. There are instances where the instruction says to use the 2nd or 3rd stitch and not the 1st. Putting it in the wrong place might only make you have an irregular shape, it might even give a result that is different from the one anticipated, and you have to reclaim the entire yarn.

- Not paying attention to U.S. and U.K. terms. Instructions might be written in either of the 2, and the onus falls on the crocheter to know which is which. If you use a U.K stitch where the instruction was written in U.S. terms, and you don't make the necessary amendments, you might end up mixing up a double crochet stitch with a single and vice versa.

- Not weaving in (fastening off) properly. This will unravel all you have done if you are not careful.

Using a Crochet Gauge

It is not uncommon for a beginner crocheter to find out that his or her crochet piece is different from the one predicted by the instructions followed. It might be bigger or smaller. A crochet gauge is a very good tool for a beginner to get the expected result.

What does a crochet gauge do? Just like the name implies, a crochet gauge "gauges" crochet projects. It specifies measurements in crochet by indicating the number of stitches per centimeter or inch.

How to Use a Crochet Gauge

1. Before you start a crochet project, look for the gauge aspect of the instructions. Read and understand it.

2. Make your base chain to be a little bit longer than the length recommended by the gauge

3. Get the correct hook size and yarn weight* by following the instructions. Yarn might be light or bulky or in between the 2. Try to get the one specified by the instruction.

Note: The weight of your yarn = the thickness of your yarn. It is NOT the weight of the ball or skein of yarn that you have. You can check the yarn pack; it should be written there.

Conclusion

Learning to crochet is a skill you will find useful because you can take what you learn and turn it into garments and projects that provide joy and utility for people who use them. With your imagination, you can take your new knowledge of the stitches and create your patterns and designs to make a variety of projects of your own.

Keep your hands relaxed so that you are not tensing up and tiring your fingers and hands. By relaxing, your stitches will come freely, and by practicing, you will be able to unravel the stitches that don't measure up to your standard, retry the stitches over and over again. You will find you like some stitches more than others.

By mastering the basic stitches, you will be able to tolerate your least favorites. The first row is always the most grueling. Make sure your foundation chain is even and not too tight. This will make it easier to fit the hook into the chain when you are making the first row of stitches. It will come easier as time goes by and you practice more.

Take the stitches you have learned and make swatches of the stitches. This practice will pay off handsomely as you perfect the stitches and grow comfortable handling crochet hooks of different sizes. Practicing is the best way to feel good about your skills. You will be able to see how much easier the stitches are made when you are familiar with how the yarn feels in your hands and how it moves along the crochet hook.

The language of crochet is defined, and the patterns are explained in plain English. Join the crochet community by putting your new skills into action. Relax and enjoy using what you learn to produce actual items that you can use and enjoy.

BOOK 2

Amigurumi Crochet Patterns for Beginners

A Step-by-Step Guide to Create
25 Cute and Adorable Animal Patterns
Through Easy-to-Follow Instructions
and Illustrations

Introduction

What is Amigurumi Crochet?

This type of crochet is said to have originated from Japan. People would use this type of crochet when making toys that would be stuffed using this crochet. Ami means knitting or yarn that has been crocheted while amigurumi means a doll that has been stuffed. This type of crochet is therefore used when one is making these stuffed dolls through the use of heavy yarn. One can also make fan items and the large novelty cushions as well as homewares.

While there are earlier records of three-dimensional knitted or crocheted dolls from China, Yoshishiro Matushita claims that in 1185, there are records of similar techniques in Japan referred to as Needle Binding. This technique is a fabric creation preceding crocheting and knitting. During the period of Edo, which was between 1603 and 1867, Japan and Netherlands traded with each other. Knitting was introduced as part of this trade.

The Samurais also initiated the evolution of knitting as they were proficient in making decorations and garments for their winter wear and katanas. During the period of Meji, which was between 1868 and 1912, Japan underwent a transition from being feudalistic into a more modernized society.

During this era, industrialization in the country began. For instance, its educational system was changed, adopting the Western education system. Thousands of Japanese students went abroad to learn Western practices while over 3,000 teachers from the West were hired to go to Japan and teach mathematics, modern science, foreign languages, and technology. Women westerners were also invited to teach needlework techniques during this period. The first stuffed crocheted work was a twigged Japanese plum with a leaf. In 1920, more fruit motifs began to appear.

Today the art of amigurumi is still a growing craft and despite being popular on online sites, such as Pinterest and Etsy, the art is dependent on popular culture, as well as emerging trends. The art depends on popular culture as well as emerging trends, yet it is very popular all over the world.

One of the most common issues that you might encounter in amigurumi is discerning the starts and ends of the round. This results in incorrect counts of stitches. To avoid this, it is best to mark the points where the round starts and ends using a locking stitch marker or a safety pin.

Most skilled crocheters use stitch markers to keep track of their stitches. If you are crocheting through the back loop alone, you will notice that you could only hold your marker on the front loop. Once you close your locking stitch marker, you would know when you are done with your next round upon reaching the marker again. Then, you only have to move the marker and set it to begin your next round.

Amigurumi Abbreviations

beg: beginning

ch: chain

dc: double crochet

lp/lps: loop/loops

rep: repeat

rnd/rnds: round/rounds

sc: single crochet

sl st: slip stitch

st/sts: stitch/stitches

yo: yarn over

cs = chain stitch

ss = slip stitch

sc = single crochet

dc = double crochet

inc = increase

dec = decrease

St(s): stitch (es).

Sc: single crochet

Ch: chain

Sl st = slip stitch

dc: double crochet.

beg: beginning

rnd: round

How to Assemble the Amigurumi

Secure with Long Tail

This means that if you are already ending your work, make sure to leave an extra length of yarn, about 6 to 9 inches. You would use this extra yarn to attach a piece of your work to another.

To attach a piece, simply thread the long tail into a tapestry needle. Then, begin stitching to the other piece. You should now have two pieces of your work secured or fastened together.

Stitch Marking

In order to hold all the pieces of your work in place, it is advisable to use locking stitch markers. As mentioned, these markers could also help in keeping track of your rounds as you crochet; however, they are also useful for holding fabrics in place.

To do this, simply place 2 stitch markers on the pieces that you are attaching to hold them in place. This way, you would be able to sew them together easily.

Stuffing the Amigurumi

The manner of stuffing your amigurumi is critical in the appearance and success of your work. You would be spending a great amount of time crocheting, which is why you want to make sure that your work will turn out great once you stuff it.

Stuffing small and large amigurumi requires different techniques. For instance, if you stuff small amigurumi, apart from being firm, the stuffing should get into all the tiny parts and pieces of the work. On the other hand, if you stuff large amigurumi, you need to learn some other tricks apart from stuffing it firmly.

For large amigurumi, you need a sufficient amount of stuffing to discern the size of your finished work. For example, if you are stuffing large animals, you want to stuff their parts, such as legs and arms in the same size. Thus, the stuffing of these parts should be in equal amounts. Prior to stuffing, it is best to set aside equal amounts of stuffing to obtain equal sizes for each arm or leg.

It is also best if you could stuff each part of your work using one big clump of stuffing rather than putting in small amounts of stuffing. The final product might look lumpy if you try to fill your amigurumi with little balls or small amounts of stuffing.

In the event that you notice that your stuffing is insufficient, it is best to add more to the center of your work. This will press out the stuffing that you put earlier to the sides of your work. Thus, it will have a smooth or flowing look. On the other hand, if you think you put in too much stuffing, you only need to take off that part that is hanging off.

These tricks apply to all pieces of amigurumi. Make sure that your final product is stuffed firmly instead of being lumpy.

Placing Equal or Similar Pieces

More often than not, crocheters opt for animal amigurumi projects. Most probably, your first amigurumi would be an animal or a doll. As such, you need to learn how to place the limbs evenly. Although this might be simple, you need to plan ahead before attaching the limbs to the entire body of your work.

If you are attaching two legs, you can attach them to the body, especially if you have crocheted through the back loop. The body would have a grid wherein you could attach the legs. In case you did not crochet through the back or your work does not have little ridge stitches, you only need to count the stitches so you can place the legs evenly on both sides of the body.

Once you have determined the proper placement of the legs or limbs, or the round in which you want to attach them, stitch along the bottom of one of the legs. Work on all sides of the leg until it is secured firmly to the round. Then, attach the second leg to the same round and do the same as you did in the first one.

It is advisable to put stitch markers so that you can hold the pieces in place. Do the same procedure if you are attaching arm pieces to the body of your work to come up with an even and symmetrical amigurumi.

Joining the Parts

Joining your amigurumi is a very important part of the process. This is also one of the most intimidating parts to conquer. When making these amigurumi animals you will have several parts that need to be attached together.

Most of them will have an end that is open (an open-ended piece) with stuffing sticking out of it just waiting to be attached to a larger body piece (a solid piece). For instance, the snout of the bear needs to be attached to the head. You want the connections of these pieces to look as neat and tidy as possible.

The first thing to do is to make sure you leave a long tail when fastening off each part. If you cut the end too short, you won't have a yarn strand long enough to sew one body part to another.

1. Take the long yarn tail from your open-ended piece and thread it through your tapestry needle.

2. Hold the two pieces that need to be stitched together in place. Make sure that you have them lined up and placed exactly where you want them. Removing and repositioning after it's been sewn together is possible but can be frustrating and messy.

3. Insert the tapestry needle through a stitch in the solid piece.

4. Now, bring the tapestry needle back through a stitch on the edge of your open-ended piece.

5. Continue to weave the tapestry needle in and out of stitches around the edge of your open-ended piece and through the solid piece until

completely closed. If you need to stuff the piece a little more before sewing everything shut, feel free to do so.

With your tapestry needle and the long loose end of the yarn, attach the ear to the head. Pinch the ear closed and weave your needle through both the edge of the ear and the head stitches at the same time, also called a whip stitch. Arms should be stitched in the same way.

Work tapestry needle under the tops of the edge stitches. Notice how the needle slides under the tops of those single crochet stitches along the edge of each piece.

Weave needle in and out along the edge and through the head stitches at the same time. Legs should be stitched in the same way.

Hold in place and position while stitching your embellishments on. Be mindful of where you are placing your needle and go slow.

Tips About Placement of Appendages

It's all about balance. Carefully place the legs so they are sticking out in a way so that your animal can sit up! In general with these patterns, this is about 7 rounds up from the bottom and 15 stitches apart.

To make the parts (like the head) less wobbly, you may want to make a second stitching lap around the place where you are attaching the head to the body with your tapestry needle.

Symmetry is important. Arms and ears should be placed evenly on either side of the head. Count rows and stitches to make sure you are attaching them in identical places.

The starting rounds of your piece will always have cleaner-looking stitches than your ending rounds. This is because the increase of stitches makes nice tight and clean rounds whereas the decrease of stitches is trickier and tends to leave larger spaces between your stitches. As such, always attach the head to the location where you close the body. That way the neat beginning rounds are facing out for all to see. There are some exceptions to this, such as with the lamb and kangaroo patterns where your last rows actually become the nose.

Make sure the leg is facing the proper direction. "Toes" should be upward. Weave tapestry needle through the top of the leg opening stitches and the bottom of the body. If you attach the legs about 7 rows up from the body, your amigurumi should be able to sit upright.

The second leg should be placed in a mirrored position from the first. Use the rounds of stitches on the body to your advantage. Make sure you are stitching to the same spot as your first leg, just on the other side of the body.

Fastening and Closing Up

When finishing the head or other parts that need to be completely closed, use your tapestry needle for the last round instead of your crochet hook. Sometimes it is difficult to get your crochet hook underneath the stitches when the rounds get small. Take your tapestry needle and weave it underneath the stitches in your final round and pull tight to close it. Then when you weave in the tail, go back through and between stitches that seem spaced out to bring them together and try to close gaps.

It is also very important that you weave in your ends well so your amigurumi doesn't fall apart, unravel, or come undone. A good rule of thumb is to weave the ends 3 times, going through the middle of the yarn fibers in opposing directions. Remember it is crucial to leave yourself enough yarn to weave in the ends properly! Don't cut those ends too short.

There is also a small shortcut you can do with amigurumi: Feel free to tuck those long ends into the inside of your project. You will still need to weave them in, but no need to clip off or make sure they are super neat if they are going to be living on the inside of your project. Push the tapestry needle through the piece to the other side, pull the yarn through and cut it, and then watch it disappear!

Stuff body to desired firmness and continue to follow the pattern to decrease with your crochet hook. Safety eyes, nose, and most other face embellishments should already be added before closing. Ears and some other features will be attached later.

Sometimes it is difficult to use your hook on the last round to close your piece. You can use your tapestry needle to work under each stitch all the way around to close the head.

Pull tightly to ensure your piece is tightly closed. Weave in your ends, so it doesn't come unraveled.

How to Weave in Your Ends

Weaving in your ends means hiding your loose ends so they don't show on your finished piece, and, in doing so, making sure they are woven in securely so your amigurumi doesn't unravel or fall apart.

You will need to weave in your ends during several parts of the process.

First, you will notice that where you started your magic ring and where you change color (like in many of the legs and arms), there will be loose ends to weave in. The nice thing about amigurumi is that a lot of the ends can be hidden inside the open-ended appendages. Secure the loose ends and then just leave them long and stuff them in with the fiberfill!

Weave your strands on the inside of the pieces with your tapestry needle a few times (no need to go overboard since they will be on the inside of your animal).

Knot the loose ends if desired and leave the ends long. No need to clip the yarn strands short with scissors. The other times you will need to weave in your ends are after you have joined the parts of the animal together and when you have finished closing a 3D piece (like the head). These loose ends will need to be woven in more carefully and neatly since they won't be hidden on the inside.

The method of weaving in your ends is pretty simple: With your tapestry needle, weave the strand into different stitches 3 to 5 times within the same color area as the yarn strand. You will want to make sure you don't weave your end in a straight line, otherwise, there is a chance your project could come unraveled. So purposely weave from different angles and directions. Pull the yarn strand tightly and snip it with scissors close to your work. Be careful not to actually cut the stitches in your amigurumi piece.

Loose ends that can be secured and stuffed into the animal's legs.

Weave like-color ends into like-color places on your project.

Ends will have to be woven in on the outside of your project when attaching limbs and closing 3D pieces.

Snip yarn end close to the project after it is securely woven in. Be careful not to cut your crochet stitches!

Face and Body Details

Most of the animals featured in this book have pretty simple faces and minimal embellishments since this is geared toward beginner amigurumi crafters. A few times you will see that you need to use your tapestry needle to stitch on face elements like the whiskers on Callie the Cat, the mouth on Benny the Bear, and the nose and mouth on Lilly the Lamb. Take your time and be careful and intentional with your stitches. Once you have the safety eyes attached in the correct spots, you can use those as the centerpiece of the face and let the other parts of the face form around it.

It helps to stitch on any details (like the whiskers) before you stuff and close the head. This will allow more room for you to work and get the details just right. It will also allow space to weave in your ends. Don't be discouraged if you feel like you need to redo the details. It takes practice!

Take your tapestry needle and a long strand of yarn in the color needed for a specific detail. Stitch through the inside of the head and back through the front of the head. Use your stitches from the head as your guide and make purposeful placements. Embroider details in the shape shown for that particular animal. End with the needle poking through on the inside of your amigurumi and weaving in your ends.

Make sure the location of the safety eye is exactly where you want it before attaching the washer to the back. You cannot move it once the washer is locked into place.

Press down firmly to attach the washer to the back of the safety eye. This goes on the inside of your amigurumi piece. When it makes a click, you know it is locked into place.

The safety nose is similar to the safety eye, just bigger. Make sure you lock it in place and then stuff your piece. You won't be able to feel or see the backside of your safety nose or eyes once the amigurumi is stuffed and put together. The nose should be placed with the point facing downward. It should be snug and secure.

Sewing Your Amigurumi

To start sewing your work, thread a tapestry needle. Make sure that you have left a long tail on the legs. Then, run the needle into the first stitch of a leg and continue until you have sewn all around the leg.

The pattern should be one stitch on a leg to one stitch on the body. Once you finish, tie a knot on the leg to fasten and do the same on the other leg. So, get started with this lovely book and become a pro at amigurumi!

Chapter 1 - Basic Stitches

This is designed to give you some of the most basic crochet stitches that are very beginner-friendly. You can use these stitches for entire projects or the basis of these stitches as a frame for more advanced stitches found later in this guide.

Single Crochet

When learning how to crochet, single crochet will become your best friend. It is the core stitch you will need to learn because it is incorporated into many crochet patterns you will come across.

The single crochet has the appearance of a very tight piece of fabric. It has very few holes in it and has distinctive uniform rows that look elegant and crisp. This gives your work a very clean look.

Heightwise, single crochet is one of the smallest of the crochet stitches; therefore, work tends to build slowly when using this stitch.

To single crochet begin with your chain or row, insert your crochet hook into the next stitch or chain along. Put your yarn over your hook and draw that yarn through the hole, once you have brought the yarn through the stitch or chain you should now have 2 loops on your hook.

Yarn over again and draw that yarn through both of these loops on your hook. You should now be left with only 1 loop on your hook, and that is it! That is how simple single crochet is.

Slip Stitch

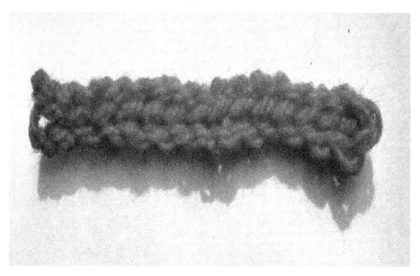

A slip stitch, like the single crochet, is one of the basics. It has a huge variety of uses and is crucial to learn early. A row of slip stitches looks very uniform and tight. This stitch is not typically used for large sheets of fabric or objects due to how tightness of the stitches.

The most common use for this stitch is for crossing a row without adding any more height to your work. It is also used to make something tighter, such as the rim of a hat. Slip stitches are commonly used to join two bits of work together, such as two sheets of fabric; to do this you work a slip stitch through both pieces of fabric to join them together.

To slip stitch insert your crochet hook into the next stitch along, yarn over and draw this yarn from back to front through the stitch, now bring that yarn through the loop that is already on your hook, and that is it! This can be a little fiddly to get the hang of, but you can make it easier by making the loop on your hook a little looser, this helps with pulling the yarn through the loop.

Double Crochet

Double crochet is twice the height of a single crochet and is just as easy. This crochet stitch has a much more open look and projects using this stitch will build very quickly. Due to the height of this stitch, you will tend to need a larger starting chain; otherwise, your work can begin to look warped.

To double crochet, begin by yarning over your hook, this will leave you with 2 loops on your hook. Insert the crochet hook into the next stitch (or 3rd stitch if starting at the beginning of a row) and yarn over once more and draw that yarn through the stitch. You will now have 3 loops on your hook. Yarn over once again and draw that yarn through 2 of the 3 loops only, once this is complete you will have 2 loops left on the hook. Yarn over a final time and draw the yarn through the last 2 loops on your hook and you are done.

Half Double Crochet

This stitch is a variant of a double crochet. The height of this stitch is the hallway between single and double crochet. This stitch has fewer steps than double crochet which makes it a favorite among many people. Another significant attribute of this stitch is that it is tall like a double crochet but has the density of a single crochet.

To make a half double crochet, begin by yarning over your hook. This will leave you with 2 loops on your hook. Insert the crochet hook into the next stitch and yarn over once more and draw that yarn through the stitch, you will now have 3 loops on your hook. At this point, all of these steps are the same as double crochet, it is how you finish the stitch that is different. Yarn over and pull that yarn through all 3 loops that are on your hook to complete the stitch, and that is it!

Treble Crochet

A treble crochet is a very tall stitch. It is commonly used for large open projects such as lightweight blankets. This stitch does require quite a few steps, but once you have mastered how to do this, it will not take very long at all. As with double crochet, you will need to compensate when turning your work by chaining 3-5 depending on the pattern.

To begin yarn over 2 times, you should start with 3 loops on your hook. Insert your hook into the stitch, yarn over and pull the yarn through the stitch giving you 4 loops on the hook. Yarn over and pull through 2 of the 4 loops on your hook, you will be left with 3 loops after pulling through. Yarn over again and pull through another 2 loops; you will be left with 2 loops on your hook. Yarn over a final time and pull through the remaining 2 loops on your hook. Yes, it is a bit time-consuming and tricky to work with, but the results are worth it.

A great way to remember how many times to pull through the loops is in the names, a single crochet only pulls through the loops once; a double crochet pulls through the loops twice, and the treble crochet will pull through the loops three times.

Front Post Double Crochet

The front post double crochet can be tricky to learn, especially if you are new to crochet. The confusion comes from the placement of your hook. The front post double crochet is simply a regular double crochet, but what makes it unique is where you will place your hook before beginning this stitch.

The finished stitch will give you the effect of a raised edge or ridge through your work. When used in conjunction with a back post double crochet, it can create a beautiful pattern. To begin do a standard row of double crochet, this is your foundation for this stitch. If the foundation is not done, the stitch will not work. Chain 2 when you reach the end of this row.

At the beginning of your new row, yarn over and instead of inserting your hook into the top of the double crochet stitch, go under and around the stitch or post itself as shown. Now yarn over and pull the yarn through the way you came. Finish off with a regular double crochet by yarning over and going through 2 loops, yarning over and going through the final 2 loops.

Back Post-Double Crochet

Like the front post double crochet, this is simply a glorified double crochet, but put into a different place to create a unique little design in your work. This stitch can be used by itself or in conjunction with the front post double crochet to create a fun raised and sunken texture within your projects.

To begin, do a regular row of double crochet to form the foundation for this stitch Chain 2 at the end of your row for turning. Now yarn over and instead of going into the top of the stitch, go behind your work and insert your hook around the post of the stitch as shown.

From this position, yarn over and pull the yarn through the path through which you came to draw up a loop. Once you have your 3 loops on the hook, yarn over and draw through 2 loops. Yarn over and pull through the final 2 loops just like in a regular double crochet. The front and back post double crochet work very well together and can create a type of stitch known as a basket weave, covered later on in this guide. These two stitches are also a perfect example of how you can take a regular basic stitch like the double crochet and alter it slightly to give you a great effect.

Front Loop Crochet

Not to be confused with the similar front post crochet, this stitch is simple and doesn't have much of an impact. The stitch can make your plain objects have a touch of pizazz with no extra effort; as it utilizes a very basic and user-friendly single crochet.

To begin, first, you need to see where your crochet hook goes. You can see from the top view of a chain or row of single crochet that you have two distinctive loops. For a regular crochet, you would use both of these loops when inserting your hook, however, for a front loop crochet, you will be going through that first loop closest to you only!

Once at this stage simply yarn over and pull through. Yarn over and go through both 2 loops on your hook exactly as you would in a double crochet, there is nothing more to this stitch, but to make more of them!

Back Loop Crochet

Just like in the front loop crochet, do not get this stitch confused with a back post double crochet as they are 2 different things. Just like the front loop crochet, this stitch utilizes the basic single crochet to create a pattern that is unique. This particular type of crochet is also used in making items like shoes and containers, as it manipulates the yarn to bend and fold in the required directions.

To begin, you need to see where your crochet hook goes, you can clearly see from the top view of a chain or row of single crochet that you have two distinctive loops.

For a regular crochet, you would use both of these loops when inserting your hook. However, for a back loop crochet, you will be inserting your hook through the back loop only. Once you have done this, yarn over as you would with a single crochet, pull the yarn through, yarn over and pull through both of the 2 loops on your hook to complete the stitch.

Moss Stitch

The Moss stitch uses 2 different crochet stitches to add a unique look to your work. This is a simple yet intriguing stitch that will spruce up many of your projects. Begin at the beginning of your row, and start by putting a regular half double crochet in that first stitch, and then slip stitch into the next stitch. Repeat this pattern of one-half double crochet and one slip stitch to the end of the row. You will be able to clearly see a little dip in your work wherever you did a slip stitch.

Once you reach the end of your row, chain 1 and turn your work. Now on this row, you want to do the complete opposite of the earlier row, this means wherever you put a half-double crochet you now want to do a slip stitch, and wherever there is a slip stitch you want to do a half double crochet.

If you forget what stitch is where, you can look at the stitch below it. If the bottom stitch is smaller than the next stitch, then it was a slip stitch, if it's higher than the next stitch, then it was a half double crochet. Keep working on this pattern until you are happy with the length of your work.

Basket Stitch

It uses both the front and back post double crochet, but in a particular pattern to create a beautiful texture to any pattern. This type of stitch is mainly used for table runners, hats and blankets. The reason is that the stitch takes a long time to complete, and the result is a dense fabric. However, you can experiment with using this stitch in any project you would like.

First, start off with the correct number of chains because this pattern relies on multiples. This means you must always have enough chains in that multiple. For example, if you decide that you want 4 stitches per basket stitch then your overall number of chains should be a multiple of 4, such as 16. If you wanted 5 stitches, then it would be a multiple of 5, such as 20. For this demonstration, we will be using a multiple of 4.

Begin by having a chain of 16 with an extra 2 for your stitch allowance. Next put one double crochet in each stitch to the end of the row, chain 2 and turn your work. At this stage, you now want to do 4 back post double crochets, and then 4 front post double crochets, repeat this pattern to complete the row, chain 2 and turn. Now repeat the pattern but this time in reverse. So, wherever you put a front post double crochet, put a back post double crochet and vice versa. Simply repeat this pattern till your work is at a length you are happy with.

X Stitch

The X stitch is a very open type of stitch.

Note: this particular stitch requires knowledge of the double crochet.

This stitch is worked over 2 stitches. Be sure your chain or row is an even number so you can fit all the stitches.

To begin, skip the first stitch and put a double crochet into the second stitch. Once you complete the first double crochet, yarn over and insert the hook into the stitch or chain that you skipped earlier.

Complete this by going around the back of the first stitch, into the stitch, yarn over and pull through before finishing off as a regular double crochet. This stitch is a little tricky to get your head around in the beginning, but it is well worth the effort as you can add a unique look to your work.

Chapter 2 - Amigurumi Patterns

Jerry the Koala

Required: 20 g of light grey acrylic, 1-2 grams of white or off-white yarn for the ears and 2 g of black yarn for the nose (I used BERNAT Premium), H hook (5 mm), a pair of 10 mm safety eyes, tapestry needle, polyester stuffing.

This toy consists of the head, body, 4 legs, 2 ears and a nose.

Head

Rnd 1. with grey yarn: 6 sc into MR (6)

Rnd 2. 6 inc (12)

Rnd 3. (sc, inc) x 6 times (18)

Rnd 4. (2 sc, inc) x 6 times (24)

Rnd 5. (3 sc, inc) x 6 times (30)

Rnd 6-10. (30)

Rnd 11. (3 sc, dec) x 6 times (24)

Rnd 12. (2 sc, dec) x 6 times (18). Begin stuffing. Insert a pair of safety eyes at round Rnd 10-11 with 8-9 stitches apart.

Rnd 13. (1 sc, dec) x 6 times (12). Add some stuffing if needed.

Rnd 14. 6 dec.

Fasten off and cut the yarn with enough length to sew it later.

Body

Rnd 1. with grey yarn: 6 sc into MR (6)

Rnd 2. 6 inc (12)

Rnd 3. (sc, inc) x 6 times (18)

Rnd 4. 18 sc in BLO

Rnd 5-12. 18 sc, Stuff as you ga

Rnd 13. (1 sc, dec) x 6 times (12). Add some stuffing to make it firm.

Fasten off and cut the yarn with enough length to sew it later.

Ears (make 2)

With white or beige yarn make 6 sc in MR, don't connect it in a circle, just turn and work from the other side to get a half-circle.

Change color to the main grey and work 6 inc (12). Fasten off and cut the yarn with enough on the end to sew it later. I usually make a double knot of 2 ends at the color-changing point and cut both ends. One more end (white) is left from the MR, I weave and cut it too (see the right ear with the weaved end before I cut it). You should end up with only 1 end of the main color for sewing (see the next picture).

Legs (make 4)

Rnd 1. with grey yarn: 4 sc into MR (4)

Rnd 2. Inc in every stitch (8)

Rnd 3. 8 sc in BLO

Rnd 4-7. 8 sc

Fasten off and cut the yarn with enough length to sew it. Stuff the details loosely

Nose (black)

With black color make 3 sc in MR, don't connect it in a circle, just turn and work from the other side to get a half-circle as for the ears.

Rnd 2. 3 sc, turn

Rnd 3. Inc, sc, inc (5). Fasten off and leave the end for sewing to the face.

Assembling

Sew the ears and the nose to the face as shown in the picture.

Attach the head to the body and all 4 limbs symmetrically, see the picture on the right showing the correct placement of the leg (view from the bottom of the toy).

Yay, your koala bear is done!

Fred the Rabbit

Fred is such an adorable little bunny that you would love to keep around the house. With perfect long ears, he is a unique gift for everyone. You can make Fred colorful, too. Just run wild with your imagination and you could have a whole family of bunnies ready to play with.

What You Need:

- DK/ worsted yarn in the color of your choice

- 4 mm crochet hook

- A pair of 6 mm safety eyes

Stuffing

Embroidery needle to sew

Head & Body

R1: 6 sc in MR (6)

R2: inc in each st (12)

R3: (sc 1, inc 1) *6 (18)

R4: (sc 2, inc 1) *6 (24)

R5: (sc 3, inc 1) *6 (30)

R6: (sc 4, inc 1) *6 (36)

R7: (sc 5, inc 1) *6 (42)

R8–14: sc in each st (42)

Attach safety eyes at R11.

R15: (sc 5, dec 1) *6 (36)

R16: (sc 4, dec 1) *6 (30)

R17: (sc 3, dec 1) *6 (24)

R18: (sc 2, dec 1) *6 (18)

R19: (sc 1, dec 1) * 6 (12)

Stuff the head and continue working the body.

R20: (sc 5, inc 1) * 2 (14)

R21: (sc 1, inc 1) * 7 (21)

R22: (sc 2, inc 1) * 7 (28)

R23–28: sc in each st (28)

R29: (sc 2, dec 1) *7 (21)

R30: (sc 1, dec 1) *7 (14)

R31: dec * 7 (7)

Stuff the body well.

Fasten off and weave in the ends.

Ears (Make 2)

R1: 5 sc in MR (5)

R2: inc in each st (10)

R3: (sc 1, inc 1) * 5 (15)

R4–5: sc in each st (15)

R6: (sc 3, dec 1) * 3 (12)

R7: sc in each st (12)

R8: (sc 2, dec 1) * 3 (9)

R9: sc in each st (9)

R10: (sc 1, dec 1) *3 (6)

FO leaving a long tail to sew.

Sew the ears to the top of the head.

Arms (Make 2)

R1: 6 sc in MR (6)

R2: (sc 1, inc 1) * 3 (9)

R3: sc in each st (9)

R4: (sc 1, dec 1) * 3 (6)

R5–8: sc in each st

FO leaving a long tail to sew.

Attach the arms to the side of the body.

Legs (Make 2)

R1: 6 sc in MR (6)

R2: inc in each st (12)

R3: (sc 1, inc 1) *6 (18)

R4-6: sc in each st (18)

Stuff the legs.

R7: (sc 1, dec 1) * 6 (12)

R8: dec * 6 (6)

R9: sc in each st (6)

FO leaving a long tail to sew. Attach the legs to the body.

Tail

R1: 6 sc in MR (6)

R2: inc in each st (12)

R3: sc in each st (12)

R4: dec * 6 (6)

FO leaving a long tail to sew. Attach the tail to the body.

Pumpkin Coffee Cozy

What You Need:

- 1 Category 4 yarn ball of medium weight yarn in Color A; here we will use Blue as Color A

- A small amount of lightweight yarn of category 4 in Color B; here we will use Orange for Color B

- A small amount of lightweight yarn of category 4 in Color C; here we will use Green as Color C

- Crochet hook of size 5.5 mm

- Crochet hook of size 3.75 mm

- Yarn needle used to thread ends

- A pair of single crochet scissors

- 1″ Button (Amy, 2013)

Cozy:

Use a crochet hook of size 5.5 mm and color A

Step 1: Make one chain 7

Step 2: Pull the loop out of the hook throughout the second ch

Step 3: Draw the loop for each of the next 4 stitches (you must be having 6 loops on the hook).

Step 4: Yarn over again and draw through all 6 loops on the hook (It's your first-star stitch) Make one chain to start closing the star (Which will be the "eye" of the star) (Amy, 2013)

Step 5: Insert your needle throughout the "eye" (ch 1 space) about your concluded star and grab the loop (2 loops on the hook)

Step 6: Introduce the hook well into the back of the last loop of the preceding star as well as draw the loop up (3 loops on the hook)

Step 7: Introduce the hook in the very same chain as the last loop of the recent star and pull the loop up (4 loops on the hook)

Step 8: For each of the next two chains, pull a loop (6 loops on the hook)

Step 9: Yarn over again and pull throughout all six loops. Make one chain to close down the star.

Reiterate steps 5-9 almost all of the way through and finish with 1 half double crochet over the last chain (same chain as that of the prior star's last loop) (6-star stitching)

Step 10: Make one chain. Ch. Switch on. Single Crochet at the top of this half double crochet.

Step 11: 1 single crochet in the "eye" of another star

Step 12: 2 single crochet in the eye for each star, all of the way through. 1 single crochet to the top of the crochet turning chain, turn this. (13 stitches)

Step 13: Chain 2, yarn over, hook in 2nd chain from hook, pull the loop up. For each of the next 3 stitches, pull a loop.

Step 14: Yarn over and pull the hook throughout all 6 loops. Chain 1 to close down the star.

Step 15: Proceed with both the star stitch (steps 5-9) almost all of the way to end with 1 half double crochet in the very same chain as the last loop of the earlier star.

Reiterate the steps form 11-15 ten times more, finishing with such a row of single crochet (I covered my cozy around my cup to decide the appropriate length. If your cozy is much too small to cover about your mug, incorporate couple more rows before you hit the perfect length).

Chain 1, switch 1 stitch crochet for each of the following 5 stitches, chain 3, skip 3 stitches, 1 single crochet in each of the final 5 stitches.

Single crochet out uniformly across the cozy whole. Fasten off with a yarn hook, and lace ends.

FOR PUMPKIN APPLIQUE:

Using a crochet hook of size F 3.75 mm and color B Magic circle.

Chain 2, 12 double crochet within a magic circle, connect in the first double crochet with an sl st (not the ch 2.)

Chain 1, [1 half double crochet, 1 dc] into the first stitches, 2 double crochet into each of the next 3 stitches, 1 half double crochet into the next stitch, slip stitch into the next stitch, 1 half double crochet into the next stitch, 2 dc into each of the next 3 stitches, [1 dc, 1 half double crochet] into the next stitch, slip stitch into the last stitch. Fasten off, and leave for weaving a long tail.

Introduce Color C in the last stitch of the previous round.

Chain 3, 1 stitch into the hook's second chain and then the next stitch, slip stitch into the preceding round's finish stitch. Fasten off and finish weaving. (Amy, 2013)

Place your embroidery into the cozy middle. Check the cozy query. Tuck your cup comfortably to evaluate where your button should be located. Sew on and you're all finished!

And now your pattern is completed

Callie the Cat

This cartoon cat character is a lovable crochet toy that you can create for your kids. You can change the colors of the yarn to make her attractive. So go ahead and have fun creating this fantastic home buddy.

What You Need:

- DK/ worsted yarn in light grey (L), dark grey (D), black (B)

- 4 mm crochet hook

- A pair of 6 mm safety eyes

- Stuffing

- Embroidery needle to sew

Body

Use L

R1: 6 sc in MR (6)

R2: sc inc in each st (12)

R3: (sc in 1 st, sc inc 1) * 6 (18)

R4: (sc in 2 sts, sc inc 1) *6 (24)

R5: (sc in 3 sts, sc inc 1) *6 (30)

R6: (sc in 4 sts, sc inc 1) *6 (36)

R7: sc in 3 sts, CC D sc in 9 sts, CC L sc in 24 sts (36)

R8: sc in 3 sts, CC D sc in 10 sts, CC L sc in 23 sts (36)

R9–10: sc in each st (36)

R11: sc in 3 sts, CC D sc in 11 sts, CC L sc in 22 sts (36)

R12: sc in 3 sts, CC D sc in 12 sts, CC L sc in 21 sts (36)

R13–19: sc in each st (36)

Attach safety eyes.

R20: (sc in 4 sts, sc dec 1) * 6 (30)

R21: (sc in 3 sts, sc dec 1) * 6 (24)

R22: (sc in 2 sts, sc dec 1) * 6 (18)

R23: (sc in 1 st, sc dec 1) * 6 (12)

Stuff the head and continue working the body R24: (dec) * 6 (6)

Fasten off and weave in the ends.

Tail

Use D

R1: 6 sc in MR (6)

R2: (sc in 1 st, sc inc 1) * 3 (9)

CC L

R3–4: sc in each st (9)

CC D

R5–6: sc in each st (9)

CC L

R7–8: sc in each st (9)

CC D

R9: sc in each st (9)

Stuff the tail.

R10: (sc in 1 sts, sc dec 1) *3 (6)

Fasten off leaving a long tail to sew.

Attach the tail to the body.

Ears (Make 2)

Use L

R1: 3 sc in MR (3)

R2: sc inc in each st (6)

R3: sc in each st (6)

R4: (sc in 1 st, sc inc 1) * 3 (9)

Fasten off leaving a long tail to sew.

Attach the ears to the top of the body.

Feet (Make 4)

Use L

R1: 3 sc in MR (3)

R2: sc inc in each st (6)

Fasten off leaving a long tail to sew.

Attach the feet to the bottom of the body.

Using B embroider a mouth and whiskers.

Sew three straight stitches above the eyes with D.

Charlie the Dog

Now, who doesn't want their favorite pet as a toy? For those who cannot keep the real ones at home, this is the best option. So, make this cuddly dog and have fun playing with him for years. With his cute tongue sticking out, he will be a great companion all day long.

What You Need:

- DK/ worsted yarn in the color of your choice

- Red yarn

- 3.5 mm crochet hook

- A pair of 4 mm safety eyes

Stuffing

Embroidery needle to sew

Head

R1: 6 sc in MR (6)

R2: inc in each st (12)

R3: (sc 1, inc 1) * 6 (18)

R4: (sc 2, inc 1) * 6 (24)

R5–9: sc in each st (24)

R10: (sc 3, inc 1) * 6 (30)

R11: (sc 4, inc 1) * 6 (36)

R12: (sc 5, inc 1) * 5, sc 6 (41)

R13: (sc 6, inc 1) * 5, sc 6 (46)

R14: (sc 7, inc 1) * 5, sc 6 (51)

R15–17: sc in each st (51)

R18: (sc 7, dec 1) * 5, sc 6 (46)

R19: (sc 6, dec 1) * 5, sc 6 (41)

R20: (sc 5, dec 1) * 5, sc 6 (36)

R21: sc in each st (36)

R22: (sc 4, dec 1) *6 (30)

R23: (sc 3, dec 1) *6 (24)

R24: (sc 2, dec 1) *6 (18)

Attach safety eyes in place. Stuff the head.

R25: (sc 1, dec 1) * 6 (12)

R26: dec * 6 (6)

Fasten off and weave in the ends.

Using black yarn, sew a nose with straight stitches.

Ears (Make 2)

R1: 3 sc in MR (3)

R2: inc in each st (6)

R3: (sc 1, inc 1) * 3 (9)

R4: sc in each st (9)

R5: (sc 2, inc 1) * 3 (12)

R6: sc in each st (12)

R7: (sc 3, inc 1) * 3 (15)

R8: sc in each st (15)

R9: (sc 4, inc 1) * 3 (18)

R10–16: sc in each st (18)

Sew the open ends using sc. FO leaving a long tail to sew.

Sew the ears to the side of the head.

Body

R1: 8 sc in MR (8)

R2: inc in each st (16)

R3: (sc 1, inc 1) * 8 (24)

R4: (sc 2, inc 1) * 8 (32)

R5: (sc 3, inc 1) * 8 (40)

R6–17: sc in each st (40)

R18: (sc 3, dec 1) *8 (32)

R19–25: sc in each st (32)

R26: (sc 2, dec 1) * 8 (24)

R27: (sc 1, dec 1) * 8 (16)

Stuff the body.

R28: dec * 8 (8)

FO leaving a long tail to sew.

Attach the head to the body.

Legs (Make 4)

R1: 6 sc in MR (6)

R2: inc in each st (12)

R3: (sc 1, inc 1) * 6 (18)

R4: (sc 2, inc 1) * 6 (24)

R5–6: sc in each st (24)

R7: sc 12, (sc 2, dec 1) * 3 (21)

R8: sc 12, (sc 1, dec 1) * 3 (18)

R9: sc 12, (dec 1) * 3 (15)

R10–21: sc in each st (15)

Stuff the legs and FO leaving a long tail to sew.

Sew the legs closed and sew them in place on the body.

Tail

Ch 10, sc in 2nd ch from hook, sc, sc, hdc in 6 sts.

FO and sew the tail to the body.

Tongue

Use red yarn

R1: Ch 4, sc in 2nd ch from hook, sc, sc

R2: Ch1, turn, inc 1, sc, inc 1

R3: Ch1, turn, sc in each st

R4: Ch1, turn, dec 1, sc, dec 1

FO and sew to the muffle.

Greg the Lion

Your wild animal collection will not be complete without the king of the jungle. This lion pattern is simple and quick to make. The orange hair crocheted around the head gives it a royal look.

What You Need:

- DK/ worsted yarn in the color of your choice

- Orange and white yarn

- 4 mm crochet hook

- A pair of 6 mm safety eyes

Stuffing

Embroidery needle to sew

Head

R1: 6 sc in MR (6)

R2: sc inc in each st (12)

R3: (sc in 1 st, sc inc 1) * 6 (18)

R4:(sc in 2 sts, sc inc 1) *6 (24)

R5:(sc in 3 sts, sc inc 1) *6 (30)

R6:(sc in 4 sts, sc inc 1) *6 (36)

R7:(sc in 5 sts, sc inc 1) *6 (42)

R8: sc in each st (42)

R9:(sc in 6 sts, sc inc 1) *6 (48)

R10: sc in each st (48)

R11: (sc in 7 sts, sc inc 1) * 6 (54)

R12–17: sc in each st (54)

R18: (sc in 7 sts, sc dec 1) *6 (48)

R19: (sc in 6 sts, sc dec 1) *6 (42)

R20: (sc in 5 sts, sc dec 1) *6 (36)

R21: (sc in 4 sts, sc dec 1) * 6 (30)

R22: (sc in 3 sts, sc dec 1) * 6 (24)

Stuff the head.

FO leaving a long tail to sew.

Mouth

Use white yarn

R1: 6 sc in MR (6)

R2: sc inc in each st (12)

R3: (sc in 1 st, sc inc 1) * 6 (18)

R4: (sc in 2 sts, sc inc 1) * 6 (24)

R5–6: sc in each st (24)

FO leaving a long tail to sew.

With orange yarn, sew a nose and with black yarn sew the lips to the mouth. Stuff the mouth and attach the mouth to the head. Attach the safety eyes just above the mouth.

Body

R1: 6 sc in MR (6)

R2: sc inc in each st (12)

R3: (sc in 1 st, sc inc 1) * 6 (18)

R4: (sc in 2 sts, sc inc 1) * 6 (24)

R5: (sc in 3 sts, sc inc 1) * 6 (30)

R6–10: sc in each st (30)

R11: (sci n 3 sts, sc dec 1) *6 (24)

R12–14: sc in each st (24)

Stuff the body.

Using the yarn left from the head sew the body and head together at the open ends.

Legs (Make 2)

R1: ch 4, sc in 2nd ch from hook, sc, 3 sc in next st, (working backwards) sc, 2 sc in last st.

R2: sc inc 1, sc, (sc inc 1) * 3, sc, (sc inc 1) * 2

R3: sc inc1, sc, sc, (sc inc 1, sc) *3, sc, (sc inc 1, sc) *2

R4: sc in each st

R5: sc in 5 sts, (sc dec 1, sc in 2 sts) * 3, sc in 3 sts

R6: sc in 5 sts, (sc dec 1, sc in 1 st) * 3, sc in 3 sts

R7–8: sc in each st

FO leaving a long tail to sew.

Stuff the legs and attach them to the body.

Arms (Make 2)

R1: 6 sc in MR (6)

R2: sc inc in each st (12)

R3–9: sc in each st (12)

FO leaving a long tail to sew.

Stuff the arms and attach them to the body.

Tail

R1: Ch 15, sc in each ch.

FO leaving a long tail to sew.

Attach to the body.

Ears (Make 2)

R1: 6 sc in MR (6)

R2: sc inc in each st (12)

R3: (sc in 3 sts, sc inc 1) * 3 (15)

R4–5: sc in each st (15)

FO leaving a long tail to sew.

Attach to the head.

Using orange yarn, cut 4 5-inch strands.

Attach these to the tip of the tail using a knot.

Hair

Use orange yarn.

R1: Ch 60, turn

R2: sc in next st, (hdc in next st, {dc, tr, dc} in next st, hdc in next st, sl st in next st) * till the end.

FO leaving a long tail to sew.

Attach the hair around the head and secure it with straight stitches.

Benny the Bear

This bear pattern is an easy one to master. With this pattern, you can go ahead and personalize it to suit various styles. So, grab your hook and yarn, and create this stunning bear. Gift it to someone special or keep it for your very own collection.

What You Need:

• DK/ worsted yarn in the color of your choice

• 4 mm crochet hook

• A pair of 6 mm safety eyes

Stuffing

Embroidery needle to sew

Head

R1: 6 sc in MR (6)

R2: sc inc in each st (12)

R3: (sc in 1 st, sc inc 1) * 6 (18)

R4: (sc in 2 sts, sc inc 1) *6 (24)

R5: (sc in 3 sts, sc inc 1) *6 (30)

R6: (sc in 4 sts, sc inc 1) *6 (36)

R7: (sc in 5 sts, sc inc 1) *6 (42)

R8–13: sc in each st (42)

Attach eyes to the head at R9

R14: (sc in 5 sts, sc dec 1) * 6 (36)

R15: (sc in 4 sts, sc dec 1) * 6 (30)

R16: (sc in 3 sts, sc dec 1) * 6 (24)

R17: (sc in 2 sts, sc dec 1) * 6 (18)

Stuff the head.

R18: (sc in 1 st, sc dec 1) * 6 (12)

R19: dec in each st (6)

Fasten off and weave in the ends.

Mouth

R1: 6 sc in MR (6)

R2: sc inc in each st (12)

R3: (sc in 1 st, sc inc 1) * 6 (18)

R4–6: sc in each st (18)

R7: (sc in 1 st, sc dec 1) * 6 (12)

Stuff the mouth.

FO leaving a long tail to sew.

Sew the mouth to the front of the head. With black yarn sew a straight stitch on R2.

Body

R1: 6 sc in MR (6)

R2: sc inc in each st (12)

R3: (sc in 1 st, sc inc 1) * 6 (18)

R4: (sc in 2 sts, sc inc 1) *6 (24)

R5: (sc in 3 sts, sc inc 1) *6 (30)

R6: (sc in 4 sts, sc inc 1) *6 (36)

R7–12: sc in each st (36)

R13: (sc in 4 sts, sc dec 1) * 6 (30)

R14: (sc in 3 sts, sc dec 1) * 6 (24)

R15: (sc in 2 sts, sc dec 1) * 6 (18)

Stuff the body.

R16: (sc in 1 st, sc dec 1) * 6 (12)

R17: dec in each st (6)

Fasten off and weave in the ends.

Sew the head to the body.

Arms (Make 2)

R1: 6 sc in MR (6)

R2: sc inc in each st (12)

R3–4: sc in each st (12)

R5: (sc in 4 sts, sc dec 1) *2 (10)

R6–7: sc in each st (10)

R8: (sc in 3 sts, sc dec 1) *2 (8)

R9: sc in each st (8)

Stuff lightly.

FO leaving a long tail to sew.

Attach the arms to the sides of the body.

Legs (Make 2)

R1: 6 sc in MR (6)

R2: sc inc in each st (12)

R3–8: sc in each st (12)

R9: (sc in 1 st, sc dec 1) * 4 (8)

Stuff lightly.

FO leaving a long tail to sew.

Attach the legs to the sides of the body.

Ears (Make 2)

R1: 6 sc in MR (6)

R2: sc inc in each st (12)

R3: (sc in 1 st, sc inc 1) * 6 (18)

R4: (sc in 2 sts, sc inc 1) * 6 (24)

R5–7: sc in each st (24)

R8:(sc in 6 sts, sc dec 1) *3 (21)

R9: (sc in 5 sts, sc dec 1) *3 (18)

FO leaving a long tail to sew.

Attach the ears to the head.

Polly the Pig

A farm won't be complete without Polly the Pig. I chose the pink color but you can choose whatever color you like to add to your farm collection.

What You Need:

- DK/ worsted yarn in pink or color of your choice 50 g

- Black yarn

- 3.5 mm crochet hook

- A pair of 6 mm safety eyes

Stuffing

Embroidery needle to sew

Head & Body

R1: 6 sc in MR (6)

R2: (inc 1, sc 1) * 3 (9)

R3: (BLO) sc in each st (9)

R4: sc in each st (9)

R5: (inc 1, sc 2) *3 (12)

R6: sc in each st (12)

R7: (inc 1, sc 1) *6 (18)

R8:(inc1, sc2) *6 (24)

R9:(inc1, sc3) *6 (30)

R10: (inc 1, sc 9) * 3 (33)

You can now attach safety eyes between R7 and R8 with 6 sts in between.

R11–19: sc in each st (33)

R20: (dec 1, sc 9) * 3 (30)

R21: (dec 1, sc 3) * 6 (24)

Stuff the pig now and continue stuffing as you go.

R22: (dec 1, sc 2) * 6 (18)

R23: (dec 1, sc 1) * 6 (12)

R24: dec * 6 (6)

Stuff well. Fasten off and weave in the ends.

Tail

Chain 20.

Sl st in the second ch from hook and in the remaining 18 chains. FO leaving a long tail for sewing.

Attach the tail to the body at the center of R24.

Legs (Make 4)

R1: 6 sc in MR (6)

R2–3: sc in each st (6)

Sl st in next st.

FO leaving a long tail for sewing. Stuff the leg.

Once you create all 4 legs, sew on the two legs at R9 with 4 sts in between the two legs at R14 with 6 sts in between.

Ears (Make 2)

R1: 3 sc in MR, ch1, Turn (3)

R2: 2 sc in each of the 3 sts (6)

R3: 2 sc in MR (8)

FO leaving a long tail for sewing.

Sew the ears at R9 with 4 sts in between.

Finishing

Using black yarn, make small straight stitches for nostrils at R2.

Baby Monsters

What You Need:

- A Size E Crochet Hook (Or Your Choice Of Hook)

- A Little Amount Of Worsted Weight Yarn

- Polyester Fiberfill Stuffing

- Plastic Safety Eyes (About 6 Mm)

White Felt

Embroidery Floss

Scissors

Craft Glue

Embroidery Needle

Yarn Needle

Pattern for the Head and Body:

To start, make an adjustable ring with an E hook and worsted weight yarn at the top of the monster's head. Chain 1 and single crochet 6 stitches through the ring, pulling it closed in the loose yarn tail.

R1 (round 1): 2 sc (single crochet) into each st (stitch) (12)

R2: * (2 sc into next st, sc into next st) rep around (18)

R3: * (sc into next st, 2 sc into next st, sc into next st) rep around (24)

R4 to R12: sc into each st (24)

Fasten off and set aside.

Pattern for the Base:

Create an adjustable ring. Chain 1 and single crochet 6 stitches into the ring, pulling it closed.

R1: 2 sc into each st (12)

R2: * (2 sc into next st, sc into next st) rep to end of round (18)

R3: * sc into next st, 2 sc into next st, sc into next st) rep to end of round (24)

Fasten off.

Instructions for the Head and Body:

Put in the hook through the ring's front, hooking the working yarn. Take out a loop into the ring.

Enfold the working yarn or the yarn from the ball throughout the hook coming from the back and pull it into the loop on the hook. You should now have a chain stitch (ch).

Single crochet 6 stitches through the ring. Through the ring's forepart, insert the hook, pulling up a loop of your working yarn to the front. You should now have 2 loops on the hook.

From the back, enfold your working yarn all through the hook, pulling into the 2 loops. You should now have 1 single crochet (sc) stitch through the ring. Then, do another 5 sc stitches into the ring.

To close the ring, take out the short yarn tail so that the stitches tighten and form a round of stitches. You should now have the baby monster's base.

In order to enlarge the round/circle, you need to increase through crocheting twice for each stitch. Beneath both the loops of the following stitch, insert the hook. Then, take out a loop. You should now have 2 loops on the hook.

Wrapping the working yarn all over the hook, pull into the 2 loops. You now have 1 sc stitch. Do a single crochet through the same area, making an increase. In most patterns, it is written as "2 sc into next st." In this round, repeat the increase for each one stitch up to 12 stitches. You may determine the number of stitches through each "v" in the circle.

For the next round, do an increase alternating each stitch. You need to put 2 stitches in the 1st stitch, which means 1 stitch in the following stitch, then 2 stitches again in the following stitch, and so forth. You should have 18 stitches once you are done with this round.

For the final round, do an increase for every 3rd stitch. You need to single crochet twice in the 1st stitch and do a single crochet again once in the next 2 stitches. Then, single crochet twice in the following stitch and so forth. You should have 24 stitches in this round.

Once you are done increasing, you should come up with a flat circle that has 24 stitches all throughout. It could become cylindrical in shape once you single stitch around through every stitch for nine rows.

Crochet around the 24 stitches use a stitch marker and move it to the loop, which is upon the hook. Do this over again until you reach 9 rows. If you prefer a taller monster, you need to have more than 9 rows. If you prefer your monster to be shorter than the specified size in this pattern, you need to do less than 9 rows.

You should now finish the body of your monster with a slip stitch through the next stitch. You need to cut the yarn, leaving a few inches and insert the hook through the next stitch. Draw out a loop and take it out all throughout the loop on the hook.

Instructions for the Base:

In order to make the monster's base, you need to do the steps from the start to create a round or circle with 24 stitches. Prior to assembling the pieces together, you need to attach the monster's eye(s) by cutting the felt piece as you prefer. You could cut it into two small circles or just one big circle. Insert the eye in the spot that you desire by cutting a small slit to secure the eye. Put it wherever you want on the monster's body and push it through. Then, place the washer into the monster's body and secure it over the eye. Make sure to push hard so the washer snaps to the body all the way down.

Then, place a small quantity of stuffing inside the monster. Make sure the bottom part fits over the body's bottom part. Using a yarn needle and the long yarn tail, stitch all the parts of the monster together. Line the stitches up and sew between them. Once the hole closes, you may insert additional stuffing as you prefer.

Design the expression of your monster using embroidery floss and a needle for stitching the eyebrows, mouth, and eyelashes. You may add other features to the face of your monster. You may add a couple of teeth by cutting and gluing a piece of felt into the mouth.

Then, you may sew or glue the edges of the eyes. Tie a strand of yarn to come up with a bow, then stitch it on the head of the monster. It is best to use yarn with the same color as the monster's head. Then, you are done!

Buddy the Elephant

Required: about 20 g of Bernat Super Value (or similar weight yarn) in light grey, 5 g of dark grey. H or C hook (5 or 2.5 mm) depending on the preferred size of the toy, a pair of 10 mm safety eyes (I have the oval ones), a tapestry needle, polyester stuffing.

The body, head and trunk are made in one detail.

Rnd 1. with grey yarn:6 sc into MR (6)

Rnd 2. 6 inc (12)

Rnd 3. (Sc, inc) x 6 times (18)

Rnd 4. (2 sc, inc) x 6 times (24)

Rnd 5. (3 sc, inc) x 6 times (30)

Rnd 6. (4 sc, inc) x 6 times (36)

Rnd 7. (5 sc, inc) x 6 times (42)

Rnd 8-17. 42 sc.

Keep working with one color if you want your elephant to be unicolored.

Or give your guy some colorful stripes while working rounds 8-17. I chose some dark grey stripes for my boy; you can go even with rainbow colors.

Rnd 18. (5 sc, dec) x 6 times (36)

Rnd 19. 36 sc

Rnd 20. (4 sc, dec) x 6 times (24). Insert safety eyes at rounds 19-20.

Rnd 21. 24 sc

Rnd 22. (3 sc, dec) x 6 times (18), Begin with stuffing.

Rnd 23-24.18 sc

Rnd 25. (4 sc, dec) x 3 times (15)

Rnd 26-27. 15 sc

Rnd 28. (3 sc, dec) x 3 times (12)

Rnd 29-30. 12 sc. Continue stuffing as you go.

Rnd 31. (2 sc, dec) x 3 times (9)

Rnd 32-33. 9 sc

Rnd 34. (Sc, dec) x 3 times (6)

Rnd 35-37. 6 sc

Rnd 38. (Sc, dec) x 2 times (4)

Make 2-3 rounds of 4 sc with no stuffing.

Ears (make 2)

Please note we will also use DC along with regular SC here

Rnd 1. with dark grey yarn: 6 sc into MR (6)

Rnd 2. 6 inc (12). Change to light grey color. The first picture shows how to properly add another color.

Rnd 3. (sc, inc) x 6 times (18)

Rnd 4. (2 sc, inc) x 6 times (24)

Rnd 5. (3 sc, inc) x 6 times (30). Change back to dark grey if you want it decolored or skip it if you prefer one color.

Rnd 6. 6 sc, (4 dc, inc) x 5 times, (36)

Fasten off and cut the yarn with a long end to sew it

Attach the ears as shown in the picture. The side with 5 sc will go to the body.

Back legs (make 2)

Rnd 1. 6 sc into MR (6)

Rnd 2. 6 inc (12).

Rnd 3. 12 sc in BLO

Rnd 4-10. 12 sc,

Fasten off and cut the yarn with a long end to sew it. Front legs are just 1 round shorter than the pair of back legs.

Stuff all legs firmly.

Tail

Combine 2 strands of dark and light grey yarn (or just 2 strands of the main color) and make ch 10.

The Elephant is done!

Holly the Hippo

Holly the Hippo is a simple yet fun pattern that you can create easily. With a large head, she demands attention from all around her. Try out various colors of yarn to make her colorful and fun to play with.

What You Need:

- DK/ worsted yarn in the color of your choice

- Pink yarn

- 4 mm crochet hook

- A pair of 6mm safety eyes

Stuffing

Embroidery needle to sew

Head

Ch 4

R1: 2 sc in 2nd ch from hook, sc, 3 sc in last ch.

Working along the back of the chain, sc, sc (8)

R2: inc 1 in first sc, inc 1, sc, inc 1, inc 1, inc 1, sc, inc 1 (14)

R3: inc 1 in first sc, inc 1, sc in next 4 sc, inc 1, inc 1, inc 1, sc in next 4 sc, inc 1. (20)

R4–7: sc in each sc (20) R8:(dec 1, dec 1, sc in next 6 sc) *2 (16)

R9: (dec 1, sc in next 6 sc) * 2 (14)

R10-11: sc in each st (14)

Stuff the body

R12: (dec 1, sc 2) * around and end with dec 1 in last 2 sc (10)

R13: dec in each st (5)

Fasten off and weave in the ends.

Body

R1: 5 sc in MR (5)

R2: inc in each st (10)

R3: (sc 1, inc 1) *5 (15)

R4: (sc 2, inc 1) *5 (20)

R5: (sc 3, inc 1) *5 (25)

R6–8: sc in each st (25)

R9: (sc 3, dec 1) * 5 (20)

R10–12: sc in each st (20)

R13: (dec 1, sc 2) * 5 (15)

FO leaving a long tail to sew. Sew head to the body.

Ears (Make 2)

R1: 6 sc in MR (6)

R2: inc in each st (12)

FO leaving a long tail to sew.

Sew ears to head.

Using pink yarn, embroider straight and stitch for nostrils.

Legs (Make 4)

R1: 6 sc in MR (6)

R2–4: sc in each st (6)

FO leaving a long tail to sew. Sew the legs to the body.

Tail

Ch 4, sl st in 2nd ch from hook, sc, sc.

Fasten off and weave in the ends.

Sew tail to body.

Dress Up

What You Need:

- Crochet Hook (4.5 Mm)

- Red Heart Comfort Yarn (Any Color) Or Yarn With The Same Weight

- Scissors

- Yarn Needle (Blunt End; For Sewing)

Abbreviations in the Pattern:

sc – single crochet

st – stitch

f/o – finish off

Note: In this pattern, every row follows a sequence. The number in the parentheses is referred to as the number of stitches that you need to achieve at the end of a specific row.

Pattern for the Dress:

R1: ch 19

R2: begin with the 2nd ch from hook; work 1 single crochet in each ch (18) ch 1 turn

R3: skip ch; work 1 single crochet in next 3 stitches; ch 4; single crochet in the 4th stitch from the beginning of ch; 1 single crochet in next 4 stitches; ch 4; sc into 4th stitch from eh beginning of ch; 1 single crochet in next 3 stitches (18); ch 1 turn

R4: skip ch; 1 single crochet in each stitch (18); ch 1 turn

R5: skip ch; 1 single crochet in next 5 stitches; 2 sc in next stitch (21); ch 1 turn

R6: skip ch; 1 single crochet in next 6 stitches; 2 sc in next stitch (24); ch 1 turn

R7: skip ch; 1 single crochet in the first stitch; ch 3; single crochet in next stitch; repeat ch 3; single crochet in next stitch until the last stitch of the row is reached; put 1 single crochet in the last stitch.

Finish off. Leave a long tail and sew the back edges together. Leave it open near the top of the dress to allow easy placement on and off the doll. Add a button of your choice. Loop to close the top.

Pattern for the Bow:

R1: ch 2

R2: work 4 sc in the 2nd chain from the hook; slip stitch in 1st stitch; pull starting yarn tail to close hole

R3: ch 2

R4: work 4 sc in the 2nd chain from the hook.

Finish off. Leave a long tail and wrap it around the middle. Knot off using the starting yarn tail.

Instructions for the Bow Strap:

Push the hook into any yarn in the bow's back, pulling the finishing yarn tail through. Ch 10 and finish off. Sew the end to the start of the chain. Weave yarn tails.

Pattern for the Purse:

R1: ch 6

R2: start in 2nd ch; work 1 single crochet in each chain (5); ch 1 turn

R3: skip ch; work 1 single crochet in each stitch (5); ch 1 turn

R4: skip ch; work 1 single crochet in each stitch (5); ch 1 turn

R5: skip ch; work 1 single crochet in each of the BLO (5); ch 1 turn

R6: skip ch; work 1 single crochet in each stitch; ch 1 turn

R7: skip ch; work 1 single crochet in each stitch

R8: ch 11; work slip stitch into the opposite corner

Finish off. Leave a long tail, fold the purse, and sew edges to close off. Weave yarn tails.

Pattern for the Overalls:

R1: ch 23

R2: start in 2nd ch; work 1 single crochet in each chain (22); ch 1 turn

R3: skip ch; work 1 single crochet in each stitch (22); ch 1 turn

R4: skip ch; work 1 single crochet in each stitch (22); ch 1 turn

Hold ends and connect with a single crochet. Use a stitch marker in the connecting stitch and move it to the last stitch you make for every completed row.

R5: work 1 single crochet in each stitch for 1 row (22)

R6: work 1 single crochet in the next 3 stitches; work 2 sc in the next stitch; repeat sequence to the last 2 stitches of the row; put 1 single crochet in the last 2 stitches (27)

R7: work 1 single crochet in each stitch for 1 row

Note: Do not break free as this would follow making the leg holes.

Instructions for the First Leg:

Use a stitch marker in the last stitch you made. The marked stitched will be the basis upon reaching the end of row 8. Skip the next 12 stitches and put 1 single crochet through the 13 stitches. You should now have 14 stitches, including the marked stitch for one leg hold.

The 13 stitches are for the other; however, they would look even when everything is done.

Work to the left. The back of the overalls should be facing you. Work 1 single crochet in each of the next 12 outer loops. Work 1 single crochet in the inner loop containing the marker. Move the marker. Work 1 single crochet in the next 13 outer loops. Do a slip stitch in both loops of the marked stitch. Finish off and weave yarn tail.

Instructions for the Second Leg:

Turn the overalls so that it faces you. Insert yarn through the utmost corner. Ch 1 and use a stitch marker onto it. Skip ch when you reach the last row. Work to the right. Work 1 single crochet in each of the outer loops for 2 rows. Do a slip stitch on both loops of the last stitch of row 11. Finish off and weave yarn tails.

Pattern for the Bib:

R1: ch 7

R2: start in 2nd ch; work 1 single crochet in each chain (6); ch 1 turn

R3: skip ch; work 1 single crochet in each stitch (6); ch 1 turn

R4: skip ch; work 1 single crochet in each stitch (6); ch 1 turn

R5: skip ch; work 1 single crochet in each stitch (6)

Finish off. Leave a long tail.

Pattern for the Straps:

R1: ch 12

R2: start in 2nd ch; work 1 single crochet in each chain (11) Finish off. Leave a long tail and weave starting yarn tail through the strap. Sew the straps to the overalls using the finishing yarn.

Instructions for the Assembly of the Overalls:

In the back of the overalls, sew 2 open ends together. Make sure to sew only the corners on the top, leaving a hole for the tail of the mouse. Weave yarn tail.

The end of each strap should be sewn to the bib. There should be enough to overlap the ends. Make sure that the overlap is on the bib's inner part to hid the overlap once the doll wears the bib.

Weave the yarn tail by the strap to the other end, stretching out the strap. Knot the yarn tail at the end. Using this yarn tail, sew the other end, then weave the other yarn tail to hide it.

Sew the bib to the center and the front of the overalls and weave yarn tails. To the back, sew the straps to the overalls. There should be a slight overlap. If you are unsure with the amount or size of the overlap, you can simply wear the overalls on the doll to measure. Weave yarn tails.

Serena the Starfish

This cute little starfish is waiting to be played with. You can create him in any color you use. This starfish is made by joining two pieces together and stuffing the whole. Sew a smile on his face and let him brighten up your day.

What You Need:

- DK/ worsted yarn in the color of your choice 50g

- Black yarn

- 3 mm and 3.5 mm crochet hook

Stuffing

Embroidery needle to sew

Body (Make 2)

Using a 3.5 mm hook

R1: 5 sc in MR (5)

R2: 2 sc in each st (10)

R3: (sc 1, inc 1) *5 (15)

R4: (sc 2, inc 1) *5 (20)

R5: (sc 3, inc 1) *5 (25)

Now change to a 3 mm hook

R6: (Ch 14, sl st into the 2nd ch from hook, sl st, 2 sc, 4 hdc, 4 dc, 1 tr, sl st in the next 4 sts of the body) * 5

R7: (1 tr in the first st on the arm, 4 dc, 4 hdc, 2 sc, 2 sl st, continue to sl st in the sts of R6 till you reach the next arm) * 5 [Figures below]

Do not FO.

Keeping the two pieces together, sl st around the edges while stuffing as you go.

Using black yarn, embroider eyes and mouth.

Casper the Octopus

Casper is a cute little octopus that you can complete in no time. A stuffed body and simple tentacles—this pattern couldn't have been easier. Choose any color you like and make her as bright as possible.

What You Need:

- DK/ worsted yarn in the color of your choice 50g

- Scraps of white yarn

- Black yarn

- 3.5 mm crochet hook

- A pair of 6 mm safety eyes

Stuffing

Embroidery needle to sew

Body

Use yarn color of your choice

R1: 6 sc in MR (6)

R2: inc in each st (12)

R3: (sc1, inc 1) *6 (18)

R4: (sc 2, inc 1) *6 (24)

R5: (sc 3, inc 1) *6 (30)

R6: (sc 4, inc 1) *6 (36)

R7: (sc 5, inc 1) *6 (42)

R8–13: sc in each st (42)

R14: (sc 5, dec 1) *6 (36)

R15: (sc 4, dec 1) *6 (30)

You can now attach the eyes between R12 and R13 with 8 sts in between. Using black yarn, sew a mouth on R14.

R16: (sc 3, dec 1) *6 (24)

R17: (sc 2, dec 1) *6 (18)

Stuff the body

R18: (sc 1, dec 1) *6 (12)

R19: dec in each st (6)

FO leaving a long tail to sew.

Tentacles (Make 8)

This is made with two pieces sewn together: one in the main color and one in white.

With white yarn:

R1: Ch 20, turn

R2: sc in 2nd ch from hook, sc in next, hdc in 17 sts FO.

Repeat the same with yarn in the main color but do not FO. Keep the pieces together and then sc in 18, 3 sc, sc in 18. Leave a long tail to sew.

Assembly

Sew the tentacles on the head around R5.

Jenny the Jellyfish

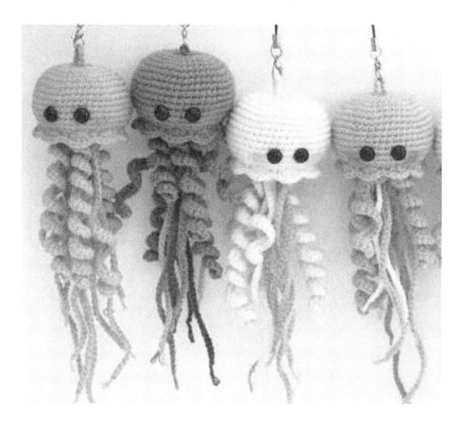

A variation of the octopus pattern, this jellyfish will be another cool addition to your collection. Make many of them in various colors. They are absolutely cute and can be used as keychains, as well.

What You Need:

- DK/ worsted yarn in the color of your choice 50g

- Black yarn

- 3.5 mm crochet hook

- A pair of 9 mm safety eyes

Stuffing

Embroidery needle to sew

Body

Use yarn color of your choice

R1: 6 sc in MR (6)

R2: inc in each st (12)

R3: (sc 1, inc 1) *6 (18)

R4: (sc 2, inc 1) *6 (24)

R5: (sc 3, inc 1) *6 (30)

R6: (sc 4, inc 1) *6 (36)

R7: (sc 5, inc 1) *6 (42)

R8–13: sc in each st (42)

R14: BLO (sc 5, dec 1) * 6 (36)

R15: (sc 4, dec 1) * 6 (30)

You can now attach the eyes between R12 and R13 with 8 sts in between.

Using black yarn sew a mouth on R14.

R16: (sc 3, dec 1) *6 (24)

R17: (sc 2, dec 1) *6 (18)

Stuff the body

R18: (sc 1, dec 1) *6 (12)

R19: dec in each st (6)

FO leaving a long tail to sew.

Skirt

Using the front loops of R14, attach yarn to any of the sts.

Ch 3, 2 dc in the same st, skip 1 sc, sc in the next, (skip 1 sc, 5 dc in next sc, skip 1 sc, sc in next) * repeat around, 2 dc in first st, sl st to top of ch 3.

FO.

Tentacles (Make 3)

Ch 31, 2 sc in 2nd ch from hook, 3 sc in every remaining st.

FO leaving a long tail to sew.

Assembly

Sew the tentacles to the center of the body base.

Wally the Whale

Wally is a tiny whale with a large heart! This quick-to-make pattern will have you creating several of them in no time. Attach safety eyes or glue on googly eyes for that impressive look. Choose colors of your choice to make Wally the Whale.

What You Need:

- DK/worsted yarn in blue and white

- 3.5 mm crochet hook

- A pair of 9 mm safety eyes

Stuffing

Embroidery needle to sew

Body

Use blue yarn

R1: 6 sc in MR (6)

R2: inc in each st (12)

R3: (sc 1, inc 1) *6 (18)

R4: (sc 2, inc 1) *6 (24)

R5: (sc 3, inc 1) *6 (30)

R6: (sc 4, inc 1) *6 (36)

R7: (sc 5, inc 1) *6 (42)

R8: (sc 6, inc 1) *6 (48)

R9: (sc 7, inc 1) *6 (54)

R10–20: sc in each (54)

R21: (sc 7, dec 1) * 6 (48)

Change to white yarn.

R22: sc in each st (48)

R23: (sc 4, dec 1) *8 (40)

R24: (sc 2, dec 1) *8 (30)

R25: (sc 1, dec 1) *8 (20)

Stuff the body

R26: dec in all st (10)

R27: dec in all st (5)

FO.

Fins (Make 2)

Use blue yarn.

R1: 6 sc in MR (6)

R2: inc in each st (12)

R3–6: sc in each st (12)

Fold and sc across to close the gap.

FO leaving a long tail to sew.

Sew the fins to the side of the body at R27.

Tail

Use blue yarn.

Make 2

R1: 6 sc in MR (6)

R2: inc in each st (12)

R3–6: sc in each st (12)

Fold and sc across to close the gap.

FO

Join the two tail pieces at the R1 edge to form a V shape tail. Sew this tail to the body at R27.

Phoebe the Turtle

Another cute pattern those kids will love! Phoebe is simple enough to create and can be either made with a single color or multiple colors. Phoebe is small in size but packs a punch. You can make him larger in size by just using larger size hooks.

What You Need:

• DK/ worsted yarn in colors of your choice (B for color1, W for color2)

• 3.5 mm crochet hook

• A pair of 9 mm safety eyes

Stuffing

Embroidery needle to sew

Body

Use B.

R1: 6 sc in MR (6)

Change to W.

R2: inc in each st (12)

Change to B.

R3: (sc 1, inc 1) * 6 (18)

Change to W.

R4: sc in each st (18)

Change to B.

R5: (sc 2, inc 1) * 6 (24)

Change to W.

R6: sc in each st (24)

Change to B.

R7: (sc 3, inc 1) * 6 (30)

Change to W.

R8: sc in each st (30)

Change to B.

R9: sc in each st (30)

Change to W.

R10: sc in each st (30)

R11: BLO (sc 3, dec 1) * 6 (24)

R12: (sc 2, dec 1) * 6 (18)

Stuff the body.

R13: (sc 1, dec 1) * 6 (12)

R14: dec in each st (6)

Fasten off and weave in the ends.

Head

Use white yarn.

R1: 6 sc in MR (6)

R2: inc in each st (12)

R3: (sc 1, inc 1) *6 (18)

R4: (sc 2, inc 1) *6 (24)

R5–7: sc in each st (24)

R8: (sc 2, dec 1) * 6 (18)

Attach the eyes at R6.

R9: sc in each st (18)

R10: (sc 1, dec 1) * 6 (12)

FO leaving a long tail to sew.

Stuff the head and sew it to the body.

Legs (Make 4)

Use white yarn.

R1: 6 sc in MR (6)

R2–3: sc in each st (6)

FO leaving a long tail to sew. Sew the legs to the body at R11.

Tail

Use white yarn.

Ch4, sl st in 2nd ch from hook, sl st, sc.

FO leaving a long tail to sew.

Sew the tail to the body at R11.

Cinderella

Materials

- A Size E Crochet Hook (Or Your Choice of Hook)

- Yarn

- Polyester Fiberfill Stuffing

- Plastic Safety Eyes (About 6 Mm)

- White Felt

- Embroidery Floss

- Scissors

- Craft Glue

- Embroidery Needle

- Yarn Needle

This pattern is a bit more difficult than the previous ones, but if you pay attention to details, you will succeed in making your very own Cinderella. There is a lot of detailing, but overall, it is a pretty straightforward pattern. You can change the details to make whatever other Disney princess you want. With different colors and a bit of difference in stitches, you can make it, I'm sure.

So, we will start off with making the head. You will use skin color for the head part. To begin, you will make a magic ring and work six sc into the ring. Then, you will increase each of the stitches. As you probably guess, you will now gradually increase the size by one

Next, we will be making the legs and the body. You will make two of the following. Using white yarn, you will make a magic ring and work six sc into the ring. Work sc around for the next five rounds. You will stuff the legs gently. Once you finish the second leg, you will leave the yarn to keep working on the body. So, in the seventh round, you will chain three and join the first leg.

Crochet six sc around the first leg, three sc in the chain three from before, six sc around the second leg and three sc on the other side of the chain three. In the next three rounds, sc all stitches. Change the color of your yarn to blue and sc all around for the next two rounds. In the 13th round, you will sc in back loops all around and in the 14th, you will sc all stitches.

Then, you will change the color of the skin and sc all around. In the 16th round, you will alternate one sc, one decrease. Then change the color to black and sc all the 12 stitches. Then, you will fasten off the yarn and stuff the body.

Next, we're making arms. Using white yarn, you will make the magic ring and sc into the ring. For the next three rounds, you will sc all around. Change color to skin and sc all around for the next three rounds. Fasten off the yarn and in doing so, leave a long tail. You don't need to stuff the arms. For the sleeves, chain nine and in the second chain from the hook slip stitch twice, sc four times and work another two slip stitches.

Fasten off the yarn. You will repeat this for the other hand and sleeve.

Next, we're going to make the hair. Using yellow yarn, you will make the magic ring and work six sc into the ring. Next, increase all around. In the third round, you will alternate one sc, one increase. In the following three rounds, you will increase by crocheting two sc, increase, three sc, increase and four sc, increase respectively.

For the next three rounds, you will sc all around. In the next round, you will skip one, crochet five double crochet (dc), skip one and you will repeat it five times. Then, you will work one sc, chain one and turn. For the next seven rows, you will work 16 sc, chain one and turn every time. Then you will fasten off the yarn with a long tail. For the bun, you will make a magic ring and work six sc into the ring.

Next, increase all around. In the next round, you will alternate one sc, one increase and in the round after you will work two sc and one increase all around. For the next five rounds, you will work sc all around. Fasten off the yarn with a long tail. For the headband, you will chain 25 using blue yarn. Next, you will do one slip stitch, three dc, two sc, one half-double crochet (hdc), 10 dc, one hdc, two sc and four slip stitches at the end. Fasten off the yarn with a long tail.

Lastly, we will make the dress skirt. Using the blue yarn you will go back to round 13 of the body. In the first round of the skirt, you will chain three in the front loops, and then repeat until the end of the round the following: four dc, two dc and slip stitch at the end of the round.

For the next four rounds, you will chain three and work dc all around, joining with a slip stitch. Fasten off and weave in the ends. For the dress band, we will use white color. Chain 26 and work one slip stitch in the second chain, then two sc, and then one hdc and one dc in the same stitch.

Then you will work one dc; two half treble crochet (htr) in the same stitch; three treble crochet (tc) in the same stitch; two htr in the same stitch; one dc; one dc, one hdc in the same stitch; one sc; three slip stitches; two sc; one hdc, one dc in the same stitch; one dc; two htr in the same stitch; three tc in the same stitch; two htr in the same stitch; one dc; one dc, one hdc in the same stitch; one sc; one slip stitch. Fasten off the yarn.

All you have to do now is to assemble the parts. Attach the head to the body. Sew on the hands and sleeves, as well as the hair, bun, headband and dress band. It is all just simple sewing on. When you're finished with sewing, weave in the ends and that's it! Congratulations!

Tommy the Crab

Tommy is a chubby little crab all ready to play with you. Make her in any color you like but red is her favorite. The pattern is a very simple one with a little bit of work on the claws. Try out this amigurumi pattern today.

What You Need:

• DK/ worsted yarn in the color of your choice

• 3.5 mm crochet hook

• A pair of 6 mm safety eyes

Stuffing

Embroidery needle to sew

Body

R1: 6 sc in MR (6)

R2: inc in each st (12)

R3: (sc 1, inc 1) *6 (18)

R4: (sc 2, inc 1) *6 (24)

R5: (sc 3, inc 1) *6 (30)

R6: (sc 4, inc 1) *6 (36)

R7–8: sc in each st (36)

R9: (sc 4, dec 1) * 6 (30)

R10: (sc 3, dec 1) * 6 (24)

R11: (sc 2, dec 1) * 6 (18)

R12: (sc 1, dec 1) * 6 (12)

R13: dec * 6 (6)

Stuff the body. Fasten off and weave in the ends.

Legs (Make 4-6)

R1: 5 sc in MR (5)

R2–7: sc in each st (5)

FO leaving a long tail to sew. Sew the legs to the body.

Claws (Make 2)

R1: 4 sc in MR (4)

R2: (sc 1, inc 1) * 2 (6)

R3: (sc 2, inc 1) * 2 (8)

R4: sc in each st (8)

R5: (sc 3, inc 1) * 2 (10)

R6: Ch 3, sc in the 2nd ch from hook, sc in next st, now working on the sts of R5—sc in each st ending with an sc under the triangular piece just made.

R7: sc 5, dec 1, sc 4 (10)

R8: sc 5, dec 1, sc 3 (9)

R9: dec 1, sc 3, dec 1, sc 2 (7)

R10: dec 1, sc 2, dec 1, sc 1 (5)

R11–14: sc in each st (5)

FO leaving a long tail to sew.

Sew the claws on the body. Sew eyes on the body at R7.

Max the Clown Fish

Doesn't Max look adorable?? Grab your supplies and let's get started on this funny little clownfish. With bright orange and white yarn and bulging eyes, Max is all set to impress you. This is an easy pattern to follow that includes color changing.

What You Need:

- DK/ worsted yarn in orange, white and black

- 3.5 mm crochet hook

- A pair of 6 mm safety eyes

Stuffing

Embroidery needle to sew

Body

Use orange yarn.

R1: 6 sc in MR (6)

R2: inc in each st (12)

R3: (sc 1, inc 1) * 6 (18)

R4: (sc 2, inc 1) * 6 (24)

R5: (sc 3, inc 1) * 6 (30)

R6–7: sc in each st (30)

R8: (sc 4, inc 1) * 6 (36)

Change to black yarn.

Place eyes at R4 with 5 sts in between.

R9: sc in each st (36)

Change to white yarn.

R10–11: sc in each st (36)

Change to black yarn.

R12: sc in each st (36)

Change to orange yarn.

R13: sc in each st (36)

R14: (sc 4, dec 1) *6 (30)

R15–16: sc in each st (30)

Change to black.

R17: sc in each st (30)

Change to white.

R18: (sc 3, dec 1) *6 (24)

Change to black.

R19: sc in each st (24)

Change to orange yarn.

R20: sc in each st (24)

R21: (sc 2, dec 1) * 6 (18)

R22: sc in each st (18)

Change to black yarn.

R23: sc in each st (18)

Change to white.

R24: sc in each st (18)

R25: (sc 1, dec 1) *6 (12)

R26: dec * 6 (6)

Fasten off and weave in the ends.

Fins (Make 3)

Use orange yarn.

R1: Ch 7, sc in 2nd ch from hook, sc in next 5 st

R2: Turn, ch1, sc in each st

R3: Turn, ch1, sc in first 2 st, dec 1, sc in last 2 sts

R4–5: Turn, ch1, sc in each st

R6: Turn, ch1, dec 1, sc 1, dec 1

FO leaving a long tail to sew.

Attach one fin to each side of the body at R12. Attach the third fin to the back of the body.

Dorsal Fin

Use orange yarn.

R1: Ch10, sc in 2nd ch from hook, sc in next 8 st

R2: Turn, ch1, sc, hdc, dc, hdc, sc, sc, hdc, hdc, sc

R3: Turn, ch1, sc, hdc, hdc, sc, sc, hdc, dc, hdc, sc

R4: sc, sc

FO leaving a long tail to sew.

Attach the fin to the top of the body.

Eyes (Make 2)

Use white yarn.

R1: 6sc in MR (6)

R2: inc in each st (12)

R3: (sc 1, inc 1) * 6 (18)

FO leaving a long tail to sew.

With the wrong side facing out, attach the safety eyes, one inside of each crocheted eye, and sew them in place on the body.

Sew a mouth using black yarn below the eyes.

Pinky the Mouse

What You Need:

- 10-15 g of any bright acrylic yarn, (I used BERNAT Premium)

- H hook (5 mm)

- A pair of 10 mm safety eyes, tapestry needle, polyester stuffing.

Please remember to leave long ends at the beginning and the end: we will use them later for Pinky's tail.

Rnd 1. with main color: 8 sc into MR (8)

Rnd 2. 8 inc (16)

Rnd 3. (sc, inc) x 8 times (24)

Rnd 4. (2 sc, inc) x 8 times (32)

Rnd 5. (3 sc, inc) x 8 times (40)

Rnd 6-10. 40 sc

Rnd 11. (3 sc, dec) x 8 times (32)

Rnd 12. 32 sc

Rnd 13. (2 sc, dec) x 8 times (24)

Rnd 14-15. 24 sc

Insert a pair of safety eyes in round 16 and begin stuffing.

Rnd 16. (4 sc, dec) x 4 imes (20)

Rnd 17. 20 sc

Rnd 18. (3 sc, dec) x 4 times (16)

Rnd 19. (2 sc, dec) x 4 times (12). Add some more stuffing if needed.

Rnd 20. 6 dec (6). Fasten off leaving a long end.

Make a few stitches with black yarn for the nose as shown in the picture

Ears (make 2)

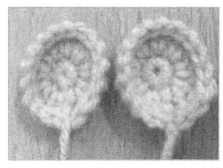

Rnd 1. Make 8 sc in MR, sl st to join and ch2 (8)

Rnd 2. 8 hdc inc, sl st to join and ch1 (16)

Rnd 3. 16 sc, sl st to join.

Tighten the MR and pull both ends (start of MR and end of work) through the whole body onto the 1st MR to form the tail later.

Sew both ears on the sides of the face as shown in the picture.

Tail

We ended up having 6 long ends coming out of the initial MR: 1 from the start and another one from the final round, where you fastened the yarn off, 2 from each ear. Take 2 ends as 1 strand and make a nice and long braided tail.

Make a few stitches with black yarn for his whiskers and our Mr. Mouse is done!

Teddy the Sloth

Required: 20 g of Bernat Super Value (or similar weight yarn) in coffee or any light brown, 5-8 g of white or off-white for the face, 5 g of dark brown for eyes pieces, H and C hook (5 and 2.5 mm) a pair of 10 mm safety eyes, tapestry needle, polyester stuffing.

We will use a smaller hook C for eye pieces.

Head

Rnd 1. with off-white yarn: 6 sc into MR (6)

Rnd 2. 6 inc (12)

Rnd 3. (sc, inc) x 6 times (18)

Rnd 4. 18 sc

Rnd 5. (2 sc, inc) x 6 times (24)

Rnd 6. 24 sc

Rnd 7. (3 sc, inc) x 6 times (30)

Rnd 8. (4 sc, inc) x 6 times (36)

Rnd 9. (5 sc, inc) x 6 times (42). Change to light brown (mail color).

Rnd 10. (6 sc, inc) x 6 times (48)

Rnd 11-14. 48 sc

Rnd 15. (6 sc, dec) x 6 times (42)

Rnd 16. (5 sc, dec) x 6 times (36)

Rnd 17. (4 sc, dec) x 6 times (30)

Rnd 18. (3 sc, dec) x 6 times (24). Begin stuffing and continue as you go.

You should make a pair of dark brown eye pieces before closing the head completely.

Rnd 19. (2 sc, dec) x 6 times (18)

Rnd 20. (1 sc, dec) x 6 times (12)

Rnd 21. 6 dec (6)

Make a few stitches to embroider the nose between the eyes as in the picture.

Eye piece (make 2 with dark brown color)

With a smaller hook (I used 2.5 mm) make chain 8

Starting from the 2nd chain from the hook make 2 sc dc, 4 dctog in the last chain. Turn to the other side of the chain and make 4 dc, 1 sc, 2 sc tog in the last loop the 1st pic below shows 4 dctog in the last chain and turn to the other side of the chain. You can see the completed 1st round on the 2nd pic.

Rnd 2. 3 sc, 4 dc, 4 dc inc in the next 4 stitches, 4 dc, 1 sc, 2 sc inc, ss in the last.

Insert your safety eyes right into the turning point of the 1st round (there's a bigger hole there) and onto the head of the sloth. Put a safety cap from inside of the head to secure it. Sew the eye pieces to the face with the narrower part pointing slightly down.

Body

Rnd 1. with light brown yarn: 6 sc into MR (6)

Rnd 2. 6 inc (12)

Rnd 3. (sc, inc) x 6 times (18)

Rnd 4. (2 sc, inc) x 6 times (24)

Rnd 5. (3 sc, inc) x 6 times (30)

Rnd 6. (4 sc, inc) x 6 times (36)

Rnd 7. (5 sc, inc) x 6 times (42)

Rnd 8-13. 42 sc

Rnd 14. (5 sc, dec) x 6 times (36)

Rnd 15. 36 sc

Rnd 16. (4 sc, dec) x 6 times (30)

Rnd 17. 30 sc. Begin stuffing.

Rnd 18. (2 sc, inc) x 6 times (24)

Rnd 19-20. 24 sc. Begin stuffing and keep doing as you go.

Rnd 21. (sc, inc) x 6 times (18)

Rnd 22-23. 18 sc

Fasten off and cut the yarn.

Arm/legs (make 4)

Rnd 1. with main color: 6 sc into MR (6)

Rnd 2. 6 inc (12)

Rnd 3. (sc, inc) x 6 times (18)

Rnd 4-6. 18 sc

Rnd 7. (1 sc, dec) x 6 times (12)

Rnd 8-20. 12 sc

Cut the yarn and fasten off leaving enough yarn for sewing. See the picture below for the correct placement of arms.

Stuff the limbs loosely and sew them to the body as shown.

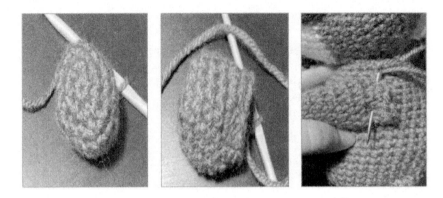

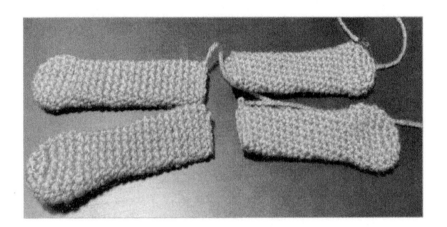

Your lazy sloth is done!

Jimmy the Owl

You can make this cute little owl with both eyes closed or open as you prefer. I've made the eyes differently to show both options for you.

Required: You will need about 10g of blue acrylic yarn for the body, a couple of grams of yellow yarn for the wings and the beak, a few grams of off-white yarn for the eyes and a few cm of black yarn if you decide to embroider the sleepy eyes (I used BERNAT Premium), 2,50 mm crochet hook (US size 2/C), a pair of safety eyes if you go with open eyes, tapestry needle, stuffing

Rnd 1. 6 sc into MR (6)

Rnd 2. 6 inc (12)

Rnd 3. (sc, inc) x 6 times (18)

Rnd 4. (2 sc, inc) x 6 times (24)

Rnd 5. (3 sc, inc) x 6 times (30)

Rnd 6. (4 sc, inc) x 6 times (36)

Rnd 7. (5 sc, inc) x 6 times (42)

Rnd 8-18. 42 sc. Stuff firmly with polyester fiberfill as you work.

Rnd 19. (19 sc. dec) x 2 times (40)

Rnd 20. 40 sc

Rnd 21. (18 sc, dec) x 2 times (38)

Rnd 22. 38 sc

Fold in half, matching each stitch on the front with the next stitch on the back, working through both sides, sc in next 21 sts, secure end.

Ear tufts (make 2)

Wrap the yarn around your 4 fingers about 10-15 times, cut the yarn leaving quite a long tail. With that tail, wrap it 2-3 times exactly in the middle, dividing it in half, make a knot to secure it.

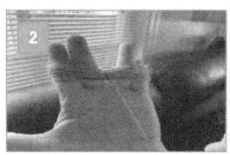 

Cut double loops on the ends of the tuft in the middle to make them fluffy as shown in the picture. Using the same yarn tail, sew each tuft on both sides of the owl's head (on the ears).

Wings (make 2)

Use yellow yarn for the wings.

Rnd 1. 6 sc into MR (6)

Rnd 2. 6 inc (12)

Rnd 3. (sc, inc) x 6 times (18)

Rnd 4. (2 sc, inc) x 6 times (24)

Cut the yarn leaving enough length for sewing, secure the end, fold the wings in half and sew them to the body.

Beak (with the same yellow yarn).

Rnd 1. 4 sc into MR (4)

Rnd 2. (1 sc, inc) x 2 times (6)

Cut the yarn leaving the end to sew the beak to the head.

All done, congratulations!

Chapter 3 – Tips and Tricks

Every crocheter requires tips and tricks to become a pro. The following tips and tricks make things easier when you begin crocheting:

Crocheting Using Thread

• When it comes to crocheting thread, remember that smaller is bigger. Threads are labeled according to their thickness. The thicker the thread, the smaller is the number. It is counterintuitive, but the more you crochet, the more you will get used to it.

• As a beginner, you can always start with a crochet thread 3, then move up to a 5 and 10. Size 20 or 30 threads can be used once you have built up your skills.

• As with the crochet threads, follow the same approach with steel crochet hooks. The smaller the size, the bigger the crochet hook. You can also look at the mm size that is usually printed on the hook itself. For example, a hook-sized 9 is 1.25 mm while the hook-sized 10 is 1.15 mm.

• As a beginner, you should start with a hook size that the pattern calls for. Once you have honed your skills a little more, you can adjust your hooks based on your comfort level and gauge.

• For beginners, it is always good to use steel crochet hooks. These hooks are much easier to use when it comes to working with thread.

• People often find crocheting using thread more difficult compared to using yarn, and it is only because of the thinner hooks involved. When you are working with the thread, all you need to do is choose a hook that has a bigger handle, that's all!

• When purchasing thread, always buy crochet thread and steer clear of embroidery or sewing thread. Although you can crochet with almost anything that resembles yarn or thread, you can make your life easier by sticking to the kind of thread that is meant for crocheting.

• When you work with yarn overs, make sure to work closely with the crochet hook head. You always want to ensure that the work on the hook is done above the segment of the hook, where it starts to get wider. Otherwise, your loops will be extremely loose.

• Another tip would be to thread around your non-crocheting hand, so it is easier to control your tension. This is extremely helpful when thread crocheting.

Crocheting Hacks with Yarn

• To prevent the balls of yarn from falling and rolling away while you are crocheting, put them in a hand wipe container. Just make sure to wash and clean it first. The yarn can be pulled through the hole of the hand wipe container.

• Use bobby pins or safety pins, or even a paper clip to mark your rows, or stitch a colored yarn or thread into the valley of the first stitch. Bobby pins and paper clips can be pulled out later once you are done.

• Use pencil boxes or jewelry boxes, or even a toothbrush holder to store your hooks.

• Use Excel sheets to map out your patterns. This is a great way to keep track of where you left off when your crocheting gets interrupted. You can also make the pattern larger to decrease eye strain.

• If you are worried about purchasing too much colored yarn that you won't be using in the future, just buy white washable yarn and dye it according to the pattern's colors.

• To keep your project in place, use yarn needles instead of hooks to weave the ends back through. This holds the project better and eliminates the chances of the yarn traveling.

• Instead of ironing your projects, which is not always ideal, mix water and starch in equal parts and spray liberally on your project; leave to dry on a flat surface.

• Keeping an index card with the lists of hooks and yarns you have is a great way to keep inventory. This ensures that the next time you are short of crochet supplies, you already know what you need.

• Yarns and other unfinished projects can be kept in zipper bags.

• It is always a good idea to keep foldable sewing scissors so that they don't snag in your crocheting bag.

• When in doubt, sew more tightly with string than you would with yarn. Try not to stitch so firmly that you hurt your hands. Knit somewhat more firmly than normal (except if you're now a skilled crocheter, at that point, simply do what you generally do!).

• Pay attention to the steps you're about to follow before you figure with thread crochet. Jumping from an acceptable hook size, worked with a cumbersome yarn all the way down to thread crochet, can make your thread paintings appear unbearably tiny. Steadily work your way down to the smaller sizes.

• Always do your crochet work in a good light so that you don't strain your eyes. This also makes crocheting easier. This is the same reason why, as beginners, you need to work with a lighter-colored thread as it makes it easier for you to find those little stitches.

• Crocheting is fun! Sure, it does have its own challenges, but that's only something you'll need to overcome at the beginning. Learning takes time, so be patient with yourself and enjoy each project you work on.

• Always choose beginner patterns when you're starting. This will make it easier for you to learn how to combine stitches and learn the ropes of crocheting.

• Working with a simple crochet swatch that uses basic stitches is always ideal, just to get the best results, minus the pressure of going through with a pattern.

Conclusion

Thank you for reading this book! Now that you have learned the basics of Amigurumi crocheting, it is time to incorporate them into the art of amigurumi. Starting with the basics is the usual thing that people do when learning a new craft or skill.

In crocheting and amigurumi, you could do various things like a cute dog or a lovely doll. However, you have to acquire a good foundation in order to do a great project. In amigurumi, learning basic crocheting is fundamental and essential.

You need to learn how to make a slip knot as it is the primary step to starting your work. After which, you could already work on various crochet stitches required for your work. It is important that you learn how to crochet through the front, back, or both loops. If you are working on the round, you should also know how to keep track of the completed stitches as well as mark the end of the round.

Crochet can be simple or as complex as you make it. In fact, as you get more and more experienced at crocheting, you will enjoy challenging yourself to create more and more projects. Creating Amigurumi crochet items is a great way of relaxing and will become second nature to you. As you practice and practice again using the images relating to the use of the crochet hook, you will soon find that this is something that you love to do and you'll work without even looking at what you are doing. It's that easy.

Amigurumi crochet is a practical and easy hobby, you can put it in your pocket and take it anywhere with you because crochet allows you to carry on your work in a moment of pause, at the bus stop, waiting for your children to come out of the school or gym, while waiting for public transportation, you can get on, sit, and pull everything out to keep working.

Besides, it is a therapy, great for soothing a tired and stressed-out mind and also it's a relaxing way to express your creativity and fill your life with colors.

As you work on a piece, for a while, you can forget your frustrations of the day and channel your mind into your work. Amigurumi Crochet is so relaxing that you will get completely lost in your new creation. When you finish for the day, your mind is refreshed.

Thank you and good luck!

Printed in Great Britain
by Amazon

27163704R00188